Heart & Life

REDISCOVERING HOLY LIVING

EDITED BY

BARRY L. CALLEN & DON THORSEN

ALDERSGATE
PRESS

Heart and Life, Rediscovering Holy Living

ALDERSGATE PRESS
THE PUBLICATIONS ARM OF

HolinessAndUnity.org

In Collaboration with
EMETH PRESS
www.emethpress.com

Library of Congress Cataloging-in-Publication Data

Heart and life : rediscovering holy living / Barry L. Callen, Don Thorsen, editors.
   p. cm.
ISBN 978-1-60947-035-7 (alk. paper)
1. Holiness. I. Callen, Barry L. II. Thorsen, Donald A. D.
BT767.H43 2012
234'.8--dc23
                   2012021475

Dedication

We dedicate this book to our friends and colleagues in the Wesleyan Theological Society who have long endeavored—in the words of Charles Wesley—to "unite the pair so long disjoined, knowledge and vital piety." Many of these men and women are represented in this book. They share valuable wisdom on how the study of Christian holiness leads to the actual living of holy lives today.

—Barry L. Callen and Don Thorsen

Contents

Introduction / 1

1. Holiness Manifesto: The Church's Great Need
   Don Thorsen / 5

PART 1. FOUNDATIONS OF HOLINESS

2. Holiness and Kingdom: the Holy Reign of God
   Howard Snyder / 17

3. Holiness and the Bible: the Proper Base
   Kenneth E. Geiger / 25

4. Holiness and Bible Reading: Beyond Mere Information
   Mark A. Maddix and Richard P. Thompson / 33

5. Holiness and Eccentricity: Finding A Useable Holiness Past
   Douglas M. Strong / 41

PART 2. EXPERIENCE OF HOLINESS

6. Holiness and Salvation: Hope for All People?
   Philip R. Meadows / 51

7. Holiness as a Second Blessing: More than Justification
   Timothy L. Smith / 59

8. Holiness and Discipleship: Saved to Serve
   Allan Coppedge / 67

9. Holiness and Spiritualities: A Range of Christian Experience
   Don Thorsen / 75

PART 3. APPLICATIONS OF HOLINESS

10. Holiness and Relevance: Facing Difficult Social Issues
    Harold B. Kuhn / 85

11. Holiness and Dis-Ability: The Paradox of Power
    Diane Leclerc / 91

12. Holiness and Women: The Empowerment of Our Foremothers
    Susie C. Stanley / 99

13. Holiness and Higher Education: The Importance of Place
    Merle D. Strege / 107

14. Holiness and Public Perception: Sanctification in
    Contemporary Films
    Thomas E. Phillips / 115

PART 4. CHURCH LIFE AND HOLINESS

15. Holiness and Worship: Focusing on God
    Henry Knight III / 125

16. Holiness and African-Americans: Holiness/Pentecostal Worship
    Cheryl J. Sanders / 133

17. Holiness and the Church: Looking Beyond Sectarianism
    Barry L. Callen / 141

18. Holiness and Unity: Fulfilling the Prayer of Jesus
    John W. V. Smith and Gilbert W. Stafford / 149

19. Holiness and World Christianity: Mission in Other Cultures
    David Bundy / 155

20. Holiness and End Times: An Optimism of Grace
    Michael Lodahl / 163

Editors, Contributors, and Original Articles / 171

Introduction

Therefore prepare your minds for action; discipline yourselves; set all your hope on the grace that Jesus Christ will bring you when he is revealed. Like obedient children, do not be conformed to the desires that you formerly had in ignorance. Instead, as he who called you is holy, be holy yourselves in all your conduct; for it is written, "You shall be holy, for I am holy" (1 Peter 1:13–16, NRSV).

The many dimensions, demands, and blessings of holiness are rediscovered in this book. To us, holiness is not an old-fashioned, outmoded concept, no longer relevant to Christians in the twenty-first century. On the contrary, we consider holiness to be as relevant today as it was for the writers of Scripture. They wrote extensively about it in relation to God and to those whom God saves. As such, holiness is "holistic." It holds together dimensions of the Christian life too often kept apart—grace and responsibility, gift and discipleship, faith and love, crisis and process, individual and social lives and responsibilities. In the following pages, it is our hope that you, the reader, will grasp both the *breadth* and *depth* of holiness for your own life.

Holiness is one of the more important realities in our understanding of who God is, of the life that God wants Christians to live and, indeed, of all the blessings of Christianity. We sing praises in church about the holiness of God. As Christians, we desire to become holy as God is holy. This desire is encouraged in both the Old and New Testaments. God views us as holy through the redemptive work of Jesus Christ; and by the work of the Holy Spirit, God acts to make Christians increasingly holy—more godly, more like Christ. It is not enough for Christ to be our Savior; he also wants to be the Lord of our lives in all that we think, say, and do.

The growth of holiness in the lives of Christians is sometimes referred to as our "sanctification"—as the sanctifying work of God's grace in our lives. While bringing the spiritual increase, God wants us to act faithfully and lovingly in response to God's sanctifying work that makes us holy. As Christians live obediently in ways described in Scripture, we are to open ourselves to holistic growth spiritually, relationally, morally, and in other ways. The apostle Paul captures the "heart and life" of God's will that we be holy when he says:

> May the God of peace himself sanctify you entirely; and may your spirit and soul and body be kept sound and blameless at the coming of our Lord Jesus Christ. The one who calls you is faithful, and he will do this (1 Thessalonians 5:23–24).

The Breadth of Holiness

For the last two decades, Dr. Barry L. Callen has served as the Editor of the *Wesleyan Theological Journal*. Dr. Don Thorsen, has served as president of the Wesleyan Theological Society and often has published articles in the journal. Now the two of us, colleagues and friends, have teamed up to provide an important resource to the church from the richness of the publishing tradition of the *Wesleyan Theological Journal*. We have been sensitive to convey significant substance without including material not easily understood outside the community of scholars—no long essays, no footnotes, etc.

The central subject of these pages is *holiness*—its definition and its practical applications. The persistent focus is on how a proper understanding and living out of Christian holiness can transform individual believers, the churches with which they affiliate, and the world in which they live. The original articles selected from the *Wesleyan Theological Journal* are reproduced here in abridged form so that the practical applications that they highlight can be easily accessible to any serious Christian reader. The articles were chosen in order to exemplify the *breadth* of holiness relevant to the world today.

The authors of these chapters are identified in the Contributors section at the end of the book. They are from a range of generations and denominations. Each is highly respected and, if yet living, has approved of the editing work done. All articles are carefully identified so that the reader may read the original version in the *Wesleyan Theological Journal* if desired. Each chapter ends with a series of questions to ponder. The concern is to make great insights from others immediately relevant to the church and world of today, and especially to you right where you live.

Our book may be used to study the biblical understanding of holiness in general; it also may be used as a devotional guide to holy living. It is as relevant to college, university, and seminary contexts as it is to adult Sunday school classes, weekday small group gatherings, or individuals interested in becoming more holy, more like Christ. It is not necessary to read through the book sequentially; each chapter is self-contained. Thus, readers may want to look at the Table of Contents and choose the chapters of most interest to them or to those whom they lead. There is more than one way to use this book beneficially, and we encourage those who read it to be creative in how they study and apply the subject matter of the growing holiness of their lives and the lives of others.

The Depth of Holiness

Those familiar with the Wesleyan, Methodist, Holiness, and Pentecostal traditions of Christianity know that these traditions consider holiness to be at the "heart" of their faith and at the core of their "life." Thus, we titled this book *Heart and Life*. It is not a new saying; for centuries Christians have promoted the phrase "holiness of heart and life" as their personal mission statement. The saying has intended to capture the *depth* of their love for God, of their thankfulness to God for salvation through Jesus Christ, of their empowerment by the Holy Spirit for spiritual growth, and of their intention to demonstrate holy love to others, individually and socially.

It is our hope that readers of this book not only grow in their knowledge of holiness, but also open their hearts and lives to God's sanctifying grace. There is an "optimism of grace" being shared in these pages with those who focus for the first time on the importance of holiness. This optimism is also being shared with those who may be *rediscovering holy living*.

Why this optimism? It grows from our belief that God *is not finished with us yet*. On the contrary, God wants Christians to keep growing and becoming more effective, individually and collectively as the church, in witnessing to God's holiness, love, and redemption. This is a holistic vision of redemption that restores people to the im-age of God in which they were created. By God's grace, may we—and you—grow in holiness of both heart and life!

Chapter 1

Holiness Manifesto:
The Church's Great Need

DON THORSEN

Focus: The "Holiness Manifesto" represents a contemporary restatement of the nature and importance of biblical holiness for Christians and the world. Don Thorsen describes the creation of the Holiness Manifesto and summarizes its wide-ranging relevance for the church and its ministries, applicable for people's physical and social needs as well as for their spiritual needs. The text of the Holiness Manifesto is included as well as a subsequent document written on the practicality of holiness beliefs and values, entitled "Fresh Eyes on Holiness." In particular, Thorsen highlights applications of holiness for Christian unity in addition to spiritual formation and worship.

The "Holiness Manifesto" is a document written in 2006 by church leaders and scholars from the Wesleyan, Methodist, Holiness, and Pentecostal traditions. It summarizes the heart of Christian holiness beliefs, values, and practices, relevant to the twenty-first century. Holiness, of course, is not a new topic; it is as old as the Bible. Yet, holiness is not always a theme to which Christians are drawn.

Authors of the Holiness Manifesto intend that it become a clarion call for the kind of salvation and lifestyle to which God calls Christians. The terminology of holiness may not be commonly used these days, but it encapsulates the totality of God's nature as well as biblical emphases upon Christian beliefs, values, and practices. As such, it serves as a unifying or ecumenical document both for Wesleyan traditions, and for other Christians, churches, and denominations concerned about holy living. Although the pursuit of Christian unity is an ongoing process, the Holiness Manifesto serves to unite disparate church and theological traditions as well as to promote the biblical emphasis upon the holiness of God and God's call for Christians to be holy.

Wesleyan Holiness Study Project

In 2003, Kevin Mannoia, then Dean of the School of Theology at Azusa Pacific University, envisioned a collaborative effort on the part of Wesleyan denominations to reconceive and promote biblical holiness for the twenty-first century. To this end, Mannoia secured from denominations the financial as well as participatory support for the Wesleyan Holiness Study Project (WHSP). The WHSP would take place over a three-year period (2004-2006). Denominations sent up to three representatives, including church leaders, scholars, and local pastors to participate in the study. Representatives at the initial meeting of the WHSP in 2004 came from the following denominations: Brethren in Christ; Church of God, Anderson, Indiana; Church of the Nazarene; Evangelical Friends Church Southwest; Free Methodist Church; Salvation Army; and Shield of Faith.

The summary document created by the Wesleyan Holiness Study Project was the Holiness Manifesto. It drew upon shorter descriptions written by participants. However, the majority of it was written by more than forty participants in the WHSP. The full text of the Holiness Manifesto follows. It is divided into three sections: The Crisis We Face; The Message We Have; and The Action We Take.

The Holiness Manifesto

The Crisis We Face. There has never been a time in greater need of a compelling articulation of the message of holiness. Pastors and church leaders at every level of the church have come to new heights of frustration in seeking ways to revitalize their congregations and denominations. What we are doing is not working. Membership in churches of all traditions has flat-lined. In many cases, churches are declining. We are not even keeping pace with the biological growth rate in North America. The power and health of churches has also been drained by the incessant search for a better method, a more effective fad, a newer and bigger program to yield growth. In the process of trying to lead growing, vibrant churches, our people have become largely ineffective and fallen prey to a generic Christianity that results in congregations that are indistinguishable from the culture around them. Churches need a clear, compelling message that will replace the "holy grail" of methods as the focus of our mission.

Many church leaders have become hostages to the success mentality of numeric and programmatic influence. They have become so concerned about "how" they do church that they have neglected the weightier matter of "what" the church declares. We have inundated the "market" with methodological efforts to grow the church. In the process, many of our leaders have lost the ability to lead. They cannot lead because they have no compelling message to give, no compelling vision of God, no transformational understanding of God's otherness. They know it and long to find the centering power of a message that makes a difference. Now more than ever, they long to soak up a deep understanding of God's call to holiness—transformed living. They want a mission. They want a message!

People all around are looking for a future without possessing a spiritual memory. They beg for a generous and integrative word from Christians that makes sense and makes a difference. If God is going to be relevant to people, we have a responsibility to make it clear to them.

We have to shed our obsession with cumbersome language, awkward expectations, and intransigent patterns. What is the core, the center, the essence of God's call? That is our message, and that is our mission!

People in churches are tired of our petty lines of demarcation that artificially create compartments, denominations, and divisions. They are tired of building institutions. They long for a clear, articulate message that transcends institutionalism and in-fighting among followers of Jesus Christ. They are embarrassed by the corporate mentality of churches that defend parts of the gospel as if it were their own. They want to know the unifying power of God that transforms. They want to see the awesomeness of God's holiness that compels us to oneness in which there is a testimony of power. They accept the fact that not all of us will look alike; there will be diversity. But they want to know that churches and leaders believe that we are one—bound by the holy character of God who gives us all life and love. They want a message that is unifying. The only message that can do that comes from the nature of God, who is unity in diversity.

Therefore, in this critical time, we set forth for the church's well-being a fresh focus on holiness. In our view, this focus is the heart of Scripture concerning Christian existence for all times—and clearly for our time.

The Message We Have. God is holy and calls us to be a holy people. God, who is holy, has abundant and steadfast love for us. God's holy love is revealed to us in the life and teachings, death and resurrection of Jesus Christ, our Savior and Lord. God continues to work, giving life, hope and salvation through the indwelling of the Holy Spirit, drawing us into God's own holy, loving life. God transforms us, delivering us from sin, idolatry, bondage, and self-centeredness to love and serve God, others, and to be stewards of creation. Thus, we are renewed in the image of God as revealed in Jesus Christ.

Apart from God, no one is holy. Holy people are set apart for God's purpose in the world. Empowered by the Holy Spirit, holy people live and love like Jesus Christ. Holiness is both gift and response, renewing and transforming, personal and communal, ethical and missional. The holy people of God follow Jesus Christ in engaging all the cultures of the world and drawing all peoples to God. Holy people are not legalistic or judgmental. They do not pursue an exclusive, private state of being better than others. Holiness is not flawlessness, but the fulfillment of God's intention for us. The pursuit of holiness can never cease because love can never be exhausted.

God wants us to be, think, speak, and act in the world in a Christ-like manner. We invite all to embrace God's call to:

- Be filled with all the fullness of God in Jesus Christ—Holy Spirit endowed co-workers for the reign of God;
- Live lives that are devout, pure, and reconciled, thereby being Jesus Christ's agents of transformation in the world;
- Live as a faithful covenant people, building accountable community, growing up into Jesus Christ, embodying the spirit of God's law in holy love;
- Exercise for the common good an effective array of ministries and callings, according to the diversity of the gifts of the Holy Spirit;
- Practice compassionate ministries, solidarity with the poor, advocacy for equality, justice, reconciliation, and peace; and
- Care for the earth, God's gift in trust to us, working in faith, hope, and confidence for the healing and care of all creation.

By the grace of God, let us covenant together to be a holy people.

The Action We Take. May this call impel us to rise to this biblical vision of Christian mission:

- Preach the transforming message of holiness;
- Teach the principles of Christ-like love and forgiveness;
- Embody lives that reflect Jesus Christ;
- Lead in engaging with the cultures of the world; and
- Partner with others to multiply its effect for the reconciliation of all things.

For this we live and labor to the glory of God.

Fresh Eyes on Holiness. At the 2007 meeting of the Wesleyan Holiness Study Project, an additional document was written in order to expand and apply the Holiness Manifesto. Participants focused upon the need for developing key themes for understanding, embodying, and proclaiming holiness in the twenty-first century. In particular, the WHSP wanted to focus on the immediate needs of pastors. Thus, a set of themes was established. The resulting document includes brief explanations of the themes that will help pastors and others to reflect upon and implement the message of holiness.

Fresh Eyes on Holiness: Living out the Holiness Manifesto

1. Dimensions of Holiness

Holiness has several dimensions. Within each dimension there are contrasting realities. It is important to embrace both elements of each contrast in order to experience and practice holiness in its completeness.

a. Individual and Corporate: We are called to be holy persons individually and to be a holy people corporately. The corporate aspect of holiness which is prominent in Scripture needs to be emphasized again in this time and culture.

b. Christ-centered and Holy Spirit-centered: The Holy Spirit's work within us leads to conformity to the person of Jesus Christ. Neither should be expressed without the other.

c. Development and End: God has an ultimate purpose for each person, which is to be like Jesus Christ. Teaching on development in the Christian life should keep the end of Christ-likeness in view.

d. Crisis and Process: A definite work of God's grace in our hearts and our ongoing cooperation with God's grace are to be equally emphasized.

e. Blessings and Suffering: Full union with Jesus Christ brings many blessings, but also a sharing of his sufferings.

    f.   Separation and Incarnation: Holy people are in but not of the world. Holiness requires both separation and redemptive, reconciling, and restorative engagement.

    g.   Forms and Essence: Holiness always expresses itself in particular forms, which are the ways in which it is translated into life and action. But the forms must not be confused with the essence of holiness itself. How do you balance these contrasting realities in your personal life and ministry? Where do you see the need for greater balance?

2. Essence of Holiness

The essence of holiness is that God is holy and calls us to be a holy people. The challenge is reflecting Jesus Christ in a relevant and contextual way that transcends social location and diversity. Indwelled and empowered by the Holy Spirit, holy people live and love like Jesus Christ. Walking intimately with him overflows in compassion and advocacy for those whom God loves.

How can you effectively embody holiness in the context where you are now, personally and in ministry?

3. Catholicity of Holiness

Although differences have led to fragmentation in churches, holiness invites unity. God wants to heal—to make whole—the brokenness of people, churches, and society. The impact of holiness goes beyond boundaries of tradition, theology, gender, ethnicity, and time to affect people and institutional structures. The resulting healing unites all Christians in wholeness, growing up into Christ-likeness. The message of holiness involves conversation and engagement with others.

What conversations and actions do you need to engage in to bring healing to people, churches, and society?

4. Holiness and Culture

Holiness people, while themselves influenced by culture, must convey the holiness message within multiple cultures. Culture affects the holiness message and churches because we are socially shaped human beings. Culture challenges us to mediate holiness in ways that are relevant and transforming without losing the integrity of the message.

How do we exegete culture and subculture in order to achieve transformation? How might you embody the holiness message in your immediate pastoral setting?

5. Holiness and Community

Individual and corporate holiness require that faith communities pursue organizational structures, processes, and content that promote radical obedience to Jesus Christ. Holiness does not develop in isolation from other believers and faith communities that provide spiritual support and accountability.

What communal structures, processes, and content would help promote radical obedience to Jesus Christ, personally and in ministry?

6. Holiness and Social Concern

Social engagement is an essential incarnational expression of personal and social holiness. It includes ministry among the poor, disenfranchised, and marginalized. Holiness requires a response to the world's deepest and starkest needs. Social engagement is the continuing work of Jesus Christ in and through the church by the Holy Spirit for the world.

Since proclamation of the gospel of Jesus Christ to the poor is essential, how do you embody the continuing personal and social engagement with the disenfranchised and marginalized?

7. Communicating Holiness

Christians live in environments of changing language. They must communicate a holiness message in ways that are clear, relevant, and winsome. The message of holiness often has been communicated with terms and paradigms that are not understood today.

What terms and paradigms could you use to communicate the holiness message in a compelling way?

Conclusion

In conclusion, let me offer three "points of light" with regard to the ecumenical potential that holiness has. They are embodied in the words of the *Holiness Manifesto*. By points of light, I mean insights about the importance of holiness recognized by people outside the historic manifestations of the Wesleyan, Methodist, Holiness, and Pentecostal traditions. Let me summarize them with the words: spirituality, ecumenism, and worship. First, holiness emphasizes the enduring concern people have to grow more intimately in their spiritual relationship with God. The Holiness Manifesto intends to provide a declaration that unites various Christian traditions of spiritual formation. Second, Christians and churches may find greater opportunities to cooperate in ministry as they focus on holiness. Ministerial cooperation represents a great way to grow in mutual understanding and appreciation for one another. Finally, holiness represents an important emphasis for how Christians and churches worship. As they focus more on holiness, their worship will become richer and more effective in witnessing to the whole gospel of Jesus Christ.

Questions to Ponder

1. How do you understand biblical holiness? How is it relevant today?

2. The Holiness Manifesto talks about the "Crisis" people face. Do you agree with its assessment of the church and world? How else would you describe the crisis?

3. The Holiness Manifesto speaks about how people have misunderstood the "Message" of biblical holiness, and that it needs to be understood in broader, more relevant ways. How else would you describe the nature and importance of holiness?

4. Based upon "Fresh Eyes on Holiness," how does holiness impact people: spiritually? physically? socially? ethically? environmentally?

5. How may holiness serve as an opportunity for cooperation and unity among Christians and churches?

PART 1

FOUNDATIONS OF HOLINESS

Chapter 2

Holiness and Kingdom: The Holy Reign of God

HOWARD A. SNYDER

Focus: Howard Snyder explores the relationship between two crucial biblical themes found in John Wesley: holiness and the kingdom of God. Holiness emphasizes the character of God and how Christians are exhorted to live holy lives. The kingdom emphasizes God's reign over all of creation. Holiness and the kingdom should not be understood only as future realities. On the contrary, they are very much present realities. The dual themes of holiness and kingdom should make believers hopeful about the ways in which God graciously wants to work in the lives of believers as well as the world, transforming both in holistic ways. Wesley and those who follow him theologically should promote these two strands of truth, seeking both God's reign and holiness.

Psalm 96 says: "Worship the Lord in the splendor of his holiness; tremble before him, all the earth. Say among the nations, 'The Lord reigns'" (96:9-10). This whole psalm is a call for all the earth to praise God as Savior and Ruler over all. "Declare his glory among the nations, his marvelous deeds among all peoples" (v.3). God reigns; He has created all things; and "he will judge the world in righteousness and the peoples in his truth" (v.13).

Though other examples might be given, these are enough to lift up what I believe is a significant biblical theme: the holy reign of God. These passages in fact tie together two themes I would like to address: the holiness of God and the kingdom (or reign) of God. My purpose is fairly simple: to explore the relationship between two biblical themes, which I believe are of concern and interest to all of us—the holiness of God and the kingdom of God. My central thesis is this: Taking these two themes together leads us to a fuller apprehension of our faith and what it means to be faithful Christian disciples in the present age.

The principal problematic of this study can be posed as a series of questions: What is the relationship between the biblical themes of the holiness and the kingdom or reign of God? In what ways does each truth help us to understand, and respond appropriately to, the other? Particularly, how might posing these questions illuminate the Wesleyan tradition?

The Holy Reign of God in Scripture

As we have seen from the references just cited, the holiness and the reign of God are intimately linked in Scripture. The Old Testament reveals a holy God who is the sovereign Ruler over all He has made. Much more could be said about this theme in the Old Testament; suffice it to say that this perspective is assumed by the New Testament writers.

Jesus and the Kingdom. It has become increasingly recognized that the kingdom of God is a key theme in the New Testament, and especially in Jesus' own life and teachings. Jesus' initial announcement was, "Repent, for the kingdom of heaven is near" (Mt. 4:17; cf. Mk. 1:15), the same message John the Baptist had proclaimed (Mt. 3:2).

The Sermon on the Mount is full of kingdom themes and kingdom imagery. The Beatitudes begin and end with references to the kingdom. The sermon includes the key injunction not to be preoccupied with food and clothing but to "seek first his kingdom and his righteousness," or justice (Mt. 6:33).

Simply looking at the biblical references, one would have to say that Jesus spoke much more about the kingdom of God than He did about the holiness of God. He did not come proclaiming God's holiness but God's reign. This assertion must be qualified, however, in two ways. First, Jesus explicitly links the holiness and the reign of God in the Lord's Prayer: "Hallowed be your name, your kingdom come, your will be done on earth as it is in heaven" (Mt. 6:9–10). Christians are to pray that God's name be held holy, that His holiness be recognized and honored, and that God's reign be manifested fully on earth.

A second qualification to my earlier statement that Jesus speaks little about the holiness of God is this: In a real sense, Jesus' whole life and teaching were an explication of God's holiness. Jesus, then, came proclaiming the kingdom of God and embodying God's holiness. He demonstrated both the power and the ethical meaning of the kingdom in His own life, death, and resurrection. Jesus empowers us with the Holy Spirit that we may live the life of the kingdom now, serving as kingdom witnesses throughout the earth.

Other New Testament References. The Apostle Paul, in his several references to the kingdom of God, links God's reign with righteousness and holiness. Perhaps the most familiar of these texts is Romans 14:17, "For the kingdom of God is not a matter of eating and drinking, but of righteousness, peace, and joy in the Holy Spirit."

In 1 Corinthians 6, Paul says, "Do you not know that the wicked will not inherit the kingdom of God? ... But you were washed, you were sanctified, you were justified in the name of the Lord Jesus Christ and by the Spirit of our God" (1 Cor. 6:9, 11). In 1 Thessalonians Paul refers to the "holy, righteous and blameless" life he lived among the people, and says he urged the believers "to live lives worthy of God, who calls you into his kingdom and glory" (1 Thess. 2:10, 12).

Summary. From the perspective of the holy reign of God, the biblical revelation may be summarized as follows: God is holy and is sovereign over all He has made. The alienation of sin constitutes a fall from God's holiness and a rebellion against His reign. Yet God continues to exercise His sovereignty over His people and among the nations. He reveals His holy character through the law, the sacrificial system, and the prophets; He exercises His sovereignty both through and in spite of Israel's kings. Jesus comes as the messianic king, embodying in himself the holy character of God. As holy God and yet finite human, Jesus offers himself as an atonement and rises in triumph over all principalities and powers. He reigns now both as head of all creation and head of the church, His body, called to live now the holy character of God. Christians are called to serve Jesus Christ as their sovereign Lord and their example for life, empowered by Jesus' Spirit among them. They are called to continue the liberating works of the kingdom which Jesus began, living in the certain hope of the final manifestation of God's reign over all things, a reign in which the holiness of God will be reflected in a new heaven and new earth of universal shalom.

The Kingdom of God in the Wesleyan Tradition

We turn now to examine the ways the kingdom of God theme has been handled in the Wesleyan-Holiness tradition, beginning with Wesley and running on through to the present.

John Wesley. For John Wesley, the key biblical text on the kingdom of God was Romans 14:17: "For the kingdom of God is not a matter of eating and drinking, but of righteousness, peace, and joy in the Holy Spirit." The reason for Wesley's preference for this text is clear: he interpreted the kingdom of God, at least, in its present dimensions, primarily in terms of the experience of sanctification in believers and especially in the community of believers.

Wesley saw the kingdom of God in terms of the present operation of God's grace in believers' lives, especially, but also in society. A progressive, dynamic understanding of salvation underlies all of Wesley's thought. Nevertheless, one detects a tension between the static and dynamic elements in Wesley. Even though he saw sanctification as dynamic and progressive, he was not entirely free of the classical Greek notion of perfection as changelessness, and salvation as the attainment of an eternal blessedness that is essentially static. This is seen also in his view of the kingdom. The kingdom is fundamentally the direct experience of God through Jesus Christ (the "kingdom of grace").

In terms of our two themes here—the holiness and the reign of God—Wesley clearly interpreted the latter in terms of the former. That is, holiness and sanctification were Wesley's chief concern, and became his paradigm for understanding the kingdom of God. One must remember, however, that for Wesley holiness named both the character of God as perfect love and the whole way of salvation (*via salutis*), embracing, in effect, a whole theology of history, or history of salvation. In this sense there is perhaps a more fundamental, historical kingdom theology in Wesley than is generally recognized.

From Wesley to the Holiness Movement. In general, in the American Holiness Movement of the nineteenth century there was a certain narrowing of focus. Specifically, the narrowing was in the doctrine of entire sanctification, and an increasingly individualizing tendency, have been noted, with at times an almost exclusive focus on the second crisis experience, in contrast to the wider sweep of Wesley's soteriological framework.

Without retracing those discussions, I would like simply to state in summary form what I see as the meaning of this transition for the themes of the holiness and the reign of God.

1. The kingdom of God played a smaller role in nineteenth-century Methodist and Holiness theology than it did in Wesley's thought. This was part of both a theological systematization (in the case of Methodism generally) and a theological narrowing (in the case of the Holiness Movement) evident in this period of transition.

2. Where the kingdom of God was treated, it was interpreted almost always in terms of holiness and the experience of entire sanctification, as was true with Wesley.

3. The question of the kingdom of God inevitably arose to some

degree in Holiness circles toward the end of the nineteenth century with the upsurge of interest in premillennialism. Discussion of the kingdom here is almost totally limited to the millennial question.

By and large, the kingdom of God was simply not a theme of nineteenth century Methodist and Holiness theology. It appears, then, that whatever stress on the kingdom of God was present in Wesley's theology largely dropped out in nineteenth-century North American Methodism.

From 1900 to Today. I would argue that in general the Holiness Movement put major stress on the holiness of God to the neglect of the kingdom of God as a central organizing theme of theology and ethics. As Holiness churches and associations moved into the twentieth century, they found themselves affected in various ways by the modernist-fundamentalist controversy, in which two radically divergent views of God's kingdom were advocated. Almost to the same degree that the Social Gospel argued that the kingdom of God was a present, this-worldly, social reality to be achieved largely by human effort, the fundamentalists insisted that the kingdom was a future reality totally dependent upon God's sovereignty. Though it would be literal and earthly in the future, its only present relevance was spiritual, other-worldly, and largely individual.

Implications for Discipleship

Finally, I believe this whole discussion of the holy reign of God suggests several implications for the meaning of Christian discipleship today. Here I am attempting to be both biblically faithful and relevant to the world in which we must live out our daily Christian commitment.

1. *Christian discipleship must be understood in terms of BOTH the holiness and the reign of God.* Both themes point to fundamental and mutually supportive biblical truths that are needed in our world today.

2. *The holiness theme accents the elements of ethics, personal experience, and Christian character* in one's conception of the kingdom of God. Holiness stresses the *character* of the God who is King, not just His power or

sovereignty. Holy, personal love becomes the controlling center, not mere power, authority, or order.

3. *The kingdom of God theme accents the broader historical, cultural, and social dimensions of holiness.* Wesley's understanding of "social holiness" makes more sense and can be more solidly grounded when interwoven with biblical kingdom themes. Here is the basis for an ethic of liberation and social transformation.

4. *Both holiness and the kingdom of God embody the "already, not yet" character of God's redemptive action.* Christians already are "saints," are being sanctified, and yet have not fully attained perfection or maturity. The kingdom of God is here, is coming, and will come. God has acted decisively in Jesus Christ, and yet continues to act through Christ the Spirit, and will act finally in the Second Coming of Christ.

5. Finally, when biblically grounded, *both themes reflect a powerful optimism of grace,* which can be a vital motive force for evangelism, social reform, and the building of authentic church life.

Much more could be said about these themes and about their interaction, but I think this overview identifies the major issues involved and the fruitfulness of accenting and combining these two strands of truth. May God help the church today truly to seek first His reign and righteousness, and to pray in faith, "May Your kingdom come, may Your will be done on earth as it is in heaven." This is the meaning of the holy reign of God.

Questions to Ponder

1. Although Christians may think about God's kingdom as being "already, not yet," that is, already present, though not yet fully present, what does it mean to think of holiness as a present reality? What does it mean to think of the kingdom of God as a present reality?

2. How have past theologies been, so to speak, overly optimistic or overly pessimistic with regard to the kingdom of God? Should Christians be more optimistic or pessimistic?

3. Why is it important to think of God's rule—God's power—in terms of holiness, righteousness, and love?

4. If holiness and the reign of God are inextricably bound up with one another, then what are the implications for the Christian life? How do holiness and God's rule relate in practice?

5. Does the holy reign of God mean that spiritual transformation is inextricably bound up with world transformation, e.g., care for the poor, advocacy against injustice, care for God's creation, and so on?

Chapter 3

Holiness and the Bible: The Proper Base

KENNETH E. GEIGER

Focus: In talking about holiness, it is essential that we begin with a biblical presentation of the nature and relevance of holiness for today. Kenneth Geiger persuasively presents the emphasis upon holiness found throughout the Bible. He begins by talking about the holiness of God, and how God wants to make people holy. God views people as holy through the justification provided by Jesus Christ, and God sanctifies them through the empowerment of the Holy Spirit. Geiger discusses both the progressive dimensions of sanctification and how a second crisis experience, subsequent to conversion, may lead to the entire sanctification of believers.

The Bible provides an authoritative basis for the doctrine of holiness. Careful exegesis under the leadership of the Holy Spirit will not only communicate with the prophetic voice of "thus saith the Lord," so much needed in our day, but will contribute a dynamic force to the message of full salvation and deliverance from both the penalty and power of sin.

The Word of God is designed, by its divine author, and is used by the Holy Spirit, not only to communicate knowledge, but is an active agent in accomplishing people's redemption. "Where withal shall a young man cleanse his way? by taking heed thereto according to thy word" (Ps. 119:9, King James Version). "Sanctify them through thy truth: thy word is truth" (John 17:17).

We are all acutely aware of the attacks being made upon the Bible as a book of authority, divinely inspired. This warfare is not new. The Bible needs not to be defended as much as it needs to be declared. This is true with respect to the Bible doctrine of holiness.

The Holiness of God

The doctrine of holiness is based upon the Bible presentation of the holiness of God: of God the Father; of Christ the Redeemer; and of the Spirit, the divine Agent in the communication of the divine nature to people.

From the very beginning God progressively revealed His holiness to people, as people were capable of understanding that holiness. The grandeur of the creation has given to people of all ages, notwithstanding the effects of the curse because of sin, a sense of awe (cf. Ps. 69). This is a step in developing the concept of the holiness of the Creator, and it accounts for the rise of the multiplied religious superstitions all over the world as people have sought peace with a force greater in power and purity than themselves.

Let us be reminded that holiness is not essentially power as expressed in the creation and other works of God; it is essentially a moral purity. Holiness is not only a principle of divine action, but it is incumbent upon His creatures. It is important that we take careful note of the Bible teaching which relates the holiness of God to people.

The Scripture passages we now examine not only set forth the holiness of God, but also the truth of the impartibility of that holiness to people. This fact is of great significance to the Bible doctrine of holiness. For example: "For I am the Lord your God: ye shall therefore sanctify yourselves, and ye shall be holy; for I am holy: neither shall ye defile yourselves with any manner of creeping thing that creepeth upon the earth. For I am the Lord that bringeth you up out of the land of Egypt, to be your God: ye shall therefore be holy, for I am holy" (Lev. 11:44, 45). "And the Lord spake unto Moses, saying, 'speak unto all the congregation of the children of Israel, and say unto them, ye shall be holy: for I the Lord your God am holy'" (Lev. 19:1, 2).

The holiness of God as taught in the Bible is not something abstract, in that it is unrelated to God's creatures. While people will always have a sense of awe and wonder as they get a glimpse of the holiness of their Maker and Redeemer, they may become a partaker of the divine nature. The Christian, purified and made holy, will passionately pray for more holiness.

It is essential to the Bible doctrine of holiness that Christ, the Redeemer, should also be holy. Holiness may be experienced by the sinner only through a holy Savior. The efficacy of Christ's atoning work is based upon the miracle of the incarnation which made possible a holy sacrifice as a "lamb without blemish." The Savior was God, and holy. Such keystone passages as John 1:1–5 must ever be kept in sharp focus.

As was true with the holiness of God the Father, the purity and righteousness of Christ the Son is impartible to people. "Therefore, if any man be in Christ, he is a new creature.... For he hath made him to be sin for us, who knew no sin; that we might be made the righteousness of God in him" (1 Cor. 5:17, 21).

The relation of the Holy Spirit to people, and His specific mission in the world to minister to people, is a well-known truth in evangelical circles. Jesus gave promise of, and prepared His disciples for the coming of the Holy Spirit. Both Jew and Gentile experienced the purification of their hearts when the Holy Spirit was given unto them. The role of the Spirit in the church, and in the maturation of the Christian, was a favorite topic of the apostles. This divine objective and possibility by grace is a distinctive of the holiness message.

People's Need

The doctrine of holiness is given perspective and purpose by the Bible's presentation of people's need. The story of sin is adequately told in the Bible. All of human history and the present world-scene attest the fact of sin and the resultant extensive total depravity of the human race.

If our doctrine of sin is unscriptural, our entire theological system will lack cohesion and purpose. Christ's redemptive purpose was to "destroy the works of the devil" (1 John 3:8). Certainly people's total need is included in the provision of His death and shed blood.

The Bible teaches the dual nature of sin, and its double cure. Sin as an act requires forgiveness, which is obtainable through repentance and faith. Sin in nature, which is inherited, requires cleansing, which is available through the power of the Holy Spirit.

In making this simple distinction between sins and sin, we need to remind ourselves that sin which remains in the nature of a regenerate believer is enmity against God, and the toleration of this sin or depravity, and the rejection of God's provision for cleansing and deliverance from it, does constitute an act of the will, and hence becomes a sin for which we are morally accountable to God. A New Testament passage which relates forgiveness for sins and cleansing from sin is 1 John 1:9: "If we confess our sins, he is faithful and just to forgive us our sins, and to cleanse us from all unrighteousness."

The answer to people's sin, both in deed and in nature, is the blood of Christ. The Holy Spirit administers the blood of atonement today, as He did on the day of Pentecost, and as He has done in all the ages past. The glorious and glad message of holiness is found everywhere throughout the Bible, and it is especially expressed in Hebrews 13:12: "Wherefore Jesus also, that he might sanctify the people with his own blood...."

Christ's Atoning Work

The doctrine of holiness is predicated upon the Bible's setting forth of the completeness and adequacy of Christ's atoning work. Full salvation as a theological term expresses a Bible precept. It presents an adequate remedy for sin, and in scope includes deliverance from the guilt, power, and ultimately the presence of sin. Christ's atoning work makes reconciliation possible, but also includes the final redemption of the body. This complete salvation is for time and eternity.

Entire sanctification is another term which applies to fullness of redemption. It is for this that Paul prays in 1 Thessalonians 5:23, "And the very God of peace sanctify you wholly; and I pray God your whole spirit and soul and body be preserved blameless unto the coming of our Lord Jesus Christ." It is evident that entire sanctification can be experienced in this life, and that following this experience it is possible to live a life of holiness and complete devotion to God.

Any detailed presentation of the Bible teaching on justification and regeneration is beyond the limits of this study. It is indeed a wonderfull experience of grace which effects in the repenting and Christ-receiving sinner the miracle of the new birth (spiritual resurrection) and imparts the blessing of forgiveness. Ephesians 2:1 and 1:7 are significant Bible references: "And you hath he quickened who were dead in trespasses and sins.... In whom we have redemption through His blood, the forgiveness of sins according to the riches of his grace."

Entire sanctification is a direct reference to the purifying work of the Holy Spirit in the heart of the believer. It is effected by the baptism with the Spirit subsequent to regeneration, and not only cleanses, but also empowers for service. Once again attention is directed to the experience of both Jews and Gentiles in the early church who experienced the "purifying of their hearts by faith" (Acts 15:8, 9). All of this is possible because of the efficacy of Christ's blood and His perfect sacrifice. His death, resurrection, and present high priestly ministry at the right hand of the Father in heaven make holiness of heart and the living of a holy life possible (see Rom. 5:1,11; 6:4–13; Col. 2:13; 3:1–4; Heb. 13:20, 21).

Ethical Content of the Bible

The doctrine of holiness is made practical by the ethical content of the Bible. Christian experience is never an end in itself. Christ's concern was not only that the Holy Spirit should come, but that those filled with the Spirit might do "the greater works." While priority is given to being, Jesus had much to say about doing. "Ye shall be witnesses unto me after that the Holy Ghost is come upon you" (Acts 1:8). The fruit of the Spirit is evidence of the Spirit-filled life. Fruit is not only beautiful, but useful.

The Bible deals with social ethics. The Ten Commandments are still in effect. A right relationship with God is coupled with a right relationship with our fellow humans. The law of love, which is the fulfilling of the whole law, includes loving God with all the heart, and our neighbors as ourselves.

Much could be said about the witness of the holy life. It is evident that with all our witnessing and evangelizing we need to give greater care to the consistency of our walk. We should emulate Paul in his ability to write to the Thessalonians, "Ye are witnesses, and God also, how holily and justly and unblamably we behaved ourselves among you that believe" (1 Thess. 2:10).

A Projection of Full Salvation

The doctrine of holiness as taught in the Bible is a projection of full salvation, which includes the initial experiences of grace, the growth or progressive aspects of the holy life, the perfection of the believer in love, a daily walk that glorifies God, preparation for the Lord's return, and the final restoration of the lost image, which includes bodily perfection through the resurrection.

We have already treated the initial experiences of grace, and have taken note of the fact that there is growth in grace after one is saved and sanctified. Christian perfection, or the perfection of love, is another subject which deserves careful study. Mention has been made of the ethical implications of holiness. The Bible does relate the work of the Holy Spirit to the church, and the preparation of the church, as the bride of Christ, for the Lord's return.

The Bible doctrine of holiness requires that all the consequences of sin and the curse must be dealt with. Christian perfection, which does not now include the perfection of the body and of performance, is the threshold of total perfection. "When we shall see him, we shall be like him" (1 John 3:2).

Conclusion

The holiness message is not based upon a few isolated proof texts. Scripture does not need to be taken out of context in order to build a foundation for the Wesleyan-Arminian theology. This great truth can be preached expositorily from several great books of the Bible.

It was a happy day in my life, after a period of confusion resulting from oft-repeated clichés, and so much theoretical preaching which was not Bible based, that the Bible itself began to speak to me and its total message was fully redemptive. The atoning work of Christ was adequate for my deepest need, for both time and eternity. This truth is so vast and so profound that we will always be reaching out to comprehend and appropriate it. I am convinced that the Bible is relevant, and that there is a Biblical basis for the doctrine of holiness.

Questions to Ponder

1. Although believers are viewed by God as holy through the atoning work of Jesus Christ, how does the Holy Spirit work to sanctify them into greater Christ-likeness?
2. In what ways should the sanctification of believers be understood ethically?
3. What do you think about the notion of "full salvation"? Is it enough for God to justify people from sin, or does God want to work more thoroughly in sanctifying the lives of believers?
4. How fully do you think God wants believers to become holy? to become Christ-like? to love God and their neighbors as themselves?
5. What should Christians do if they want to become more holy? How may the process of sanctification be enhanced by a second crisis experience, subsequent to conversion?

Chapter 4

Holiness and Bible Reading: Beyond Mere Information

MARK A. MADDIX AND RICHARD P. THOMPSON

Focus: Is the Bible losing ground in its authoritative impact on today's Christians? If so, a large part of the problem may be that it is being read mainly to gain the building blocks of "assured doctrine." Such can be an arid, theoretical, mechanical, even boring process. But, according to Mark Maddix and Richard Thompson, reading the Bible properly should be an adventure with God's Spirit in the process of our becoming all that God intends today. It should be an exercise in seeking our greater holiness fulfillment. The primary point of the reading should not be the mere gathering of religious information, but being formed into holy people active in the world for holy purposes.

John Wesley described himself as *homo unius libri*, "a man of one book." Christians generally continue to voice strong assertions regarding the authority of the Bible. Even so, in recent years the use of the Bible within the church has tended to decrease in importance. When one considers the church's contemporary formative practices (e.g., worship) and concerns for discipleship, we see increasingly the Bible's role being limited to the realm of establishing the elements of Christian doctrine.

Some blame for this trend may fall on the church's dependence on the preferred approaches to the Bible that have largely characterized traditional biblical scholarship during the last two centuries. The general trends of biblical scholarship in the modern era have focused on "what the text meant" since all biblical texts were written in and to particular historical contexts. This may leave today's interpreter starving for even a few crumbs of some illusive message that engages the present and enables a current hearing of God's voice.

We explore here the role of the Bible as sacred Scripture within the context of the church and then also how the biblical texts may be appropriated and function within that church context in terms of *formation* and *transformation*, rather than merely in terms of *information*. We consider (1) the historic role of the Bible as sacred Scripture within the church and then (2) ways that the Bible as sacred Scripture forms and transforms Christians into faithful disciples within the context of today's church. First, what did the Bible mean originally? Second, what does the Bible mean and enable now to assist in actually shaping Christian life?

The Formative Role of the Bible

Historically, there is a difference between interpreting the *Bible* and interpreting these same texts as *Scripture*. The common assumption is that the role of the Bible is to enable us to assess the validity of Christian doctrine by what the Bible states. The text functions to clarify theological *information* about the Christian faith. However, the process by which the Bible itself was gathered and approved as "official" suggests that the incorporation of particular writings had more to do with their *formative* rather than their purely informational role. That is, the early church turned repeatedly to this particular collection of texts because of the formative ways that these texts (and not others) functioned within the Christian community on behalf of the growth of believers.

One may perceive this formative understanding of the Bible *as Scripture* in the writings of John Wesley. He declared that he read the Bible "to find the way to heaven." He did not focus on heaven as a goal or ideal *per se,* but instead on the "way" that leads to the life of salvation. Thus, the Bible functions as sacred Scripture in the various ways that these texts function to transform and shape the perspectives and lives of those who comprise the church, not simply by supplying arguments that someone may use to validate the reliability of the Bible and its various teachings.

An understanding of the formative role of Scripture suggests that there is more to the process of Bible interpretation than the discovery of an historical meaning contained in a biblical text. The criterion for the perception of these biblical texts as authoritative Scripture is not merely what these texts *state* (i.e., in the information provided by these texts) but what these texts *do* (i.e., the ways that these texts function to affect their readers).

As important as the biblical text before Christian readers may be, something essential beyond the information in the text must happen within these readers so that this text becomes *Scripture* for them. There must be a convergence of the text and its readers that brings those otherwise dead words to life. For instance, John Wesley stressed the essential role of the Spirit in the inspiration of Christian readers so that they might think about and discern the will of God through a particular text of Scripture. The partners in the reading of Scripture, the reader and the Spirit of God, contribute to what may be described as "inspired imagination." This enables readers to discover potential meanings about God and God's ongoing saving activities in today's world.

An understanding of the formative role of Scripture suggests that the church should be a primary location where these texts are probed and then function authoritatively. In significant ways, the Christian Scriptures assume the confessional context within which the reading and interpretation of these texts is expected to occur. Such a corporate context invites all who comprise the church to the reading table, lay-persons and scholars, leaders and theologians, to consider how the text may speak to the contemporary context.

An understanding of the formative role of Scripture in the church's life suggests the necessity of *living out* the engagement with these texts as Scripture. For Wesley, to speak about the authority of Scripture meant that one must also consider the church's mission and practices that encourage and incite holy living among its people. Therefore, the Bible functions in authoritative ways as sacred Scripture when the church engages the biblical texts so that Christians do not simply talk or write about what these texts may have to say, but rather *actively respond* in potentially faithful ways to the God about whom these texts speak and who speaks to the church through them. To grant the Bible its proper authority involves reading it in cooperation with the Spirit's present ministry.

Avenues for Forming Christians into Faithful Disciples

Formational reading of Scripture involves opening oneself to the biblical text, allowing it to intrude into one's life, to be addressed and encountered by it. Instead of mastering the text through study, formational reading invites that text as sacred Scripture to master and form its readers. Spiritual reading is a meditative approach to the written word. It requires unhurried time and an open heart. The purpose of reading is that God may address the faithful reader. In order for this to take place, it requires both the practice of attentive listening and a willingness to respond to what one hears.

Since the Bible does more than inform but also forms and trans-forms, Christians are to develop appropriate avenues to enable them to grow as faithful disciples. The point is not the mere gathering of religious information, but *being formed into holy people* active in the world for holy purposes. Three major areas in which Scripture functions formatively are explored here: *lectio divina*, inductive Bible study, and worship (preaching, Scripture reading, and communion).

1. *Lectio Divina.* This is an ancient process in church life, one of scriptural encounter that includes a series of prayer dynamics that move the reader to a deep level of engagement with the chosen text and with the Spirit who enlivens the text. It begins with *silencio* (silence), as one approaches a biblical passage in open, receptive, listening, and silent reading. The next step is *lectio* (reading), which is to read the text aloud, slowly and deliberately, to evoke imagination. Hearing the text read reminds the hearer of the spoken word of God. Following this reading is a time of meditation. To meditate is to think about or mentally chew on what has been read. In the past, this process often included the commitment of the text to memory. By internalizing the text in its verbal form, one passes on to a rumination or mediation on its meaning (*meditatio*).

Because the text is engaged in experiential terms, the mediation gives rise to prayer (*ortio*) or response to God, who speaks in and through the text. Next, through fervent prayer one may reach that degree of union with God through the Spirit that results in contemplation. In *contemplatio* (contemplation) the person stops and rests silently before God, receiving whatever the Spirit gives. The final step of sacred reading is *compassio* (compassion), which is the fruit of the contemplation of God as love, love of God and neighbor.

2. Small Groups. Meditative Bible study often occurs best in small groups of serious disciples. For people with a limited knowledge of the Bible, reading and studying the Bible as Scripture in the context of an intimate group gives opportunities for learning and spiritual growth. Spiritual formation and growth always take place within a social context. The Christian life is not a solitary journey, but a pilgrimage made in the company of other believers. Studying the Bible in a small group helps people broaden and deepen their understanding of a given passage, while potentially guarding against misleading individual interpretations (which is one of many reasons why biblical interpretation needs to take place in the context of community).

John Wesley has been called the "father" of the modern small-group concept. He employed a methodical approach to spiritual formation that focused on assisting participants to grow in holiness of heart and life. Wesley's group formation process incorporated Scripture as central. The reading, interpretation, and proclamation of Scripture were normal aspects of society meetings; the use of Scripture in shaping behavior and holy living was a formative aspect of classes and bands. A Wesleyan approach to Bible study does not begin with deductive presuppositions *per se*, but rather seeks inductively a creative encounter with God through Scripture, which takes the faithful reader to a deeper level of understanding and experience than simply the gathering of factual information.

As faithful disciples gather in small groups for Bible study, the Holy Spirit is active in the community to form and shape faithful disciples. Bible study incites readers to discern the deep meaning of the text and its implications for daily life. The practice of inductive Bible study, both personally and corporately, is a means of grace. Congregations that see the Bible in active dialogue with the church seek to discern not only the questions they raise about the text but also the questions the text as Scripture raises about the holiness of the reader and the life of the church.

3. Scripture in Preaching and Worship. Christians can encounter the transforming power of the Bible through a variety of worship practices. First, Christians engage Scripture through the preaching of the Word. Historically, preaching in the early church preceded the writing of the New Testament texts. The eyewitnesses of the Christ event testified to what they had seen and heard. Preaching touched and transformed the lives of the early Christians.

In similar ways, when the Scripture is preached today, the hope is that lives are changed through the work of the Holy Spirit. The proclamation of Scripture emphasizes the spoken Word of God that bears witness to the incarnate Word of Jesus Christ. But there is more to this than bearing witness. Through the proclamation of Scripture, the spoken Word becomes a fresh expression of the living and active Word of God. In this sense, the spoken word becomes a "means of grace." The preacher speaks *for* God, *from* the Scriptures, *by* authority from the church, *to* the people. God speaks through the proclamation of the Word, through the inspiration of Scripture, to provide healing and reconciliation. The preacher interprets Scripture for the community, placing it within the larger narrative of the biblical witness, and helps congregants find meaning for life.

Beyond preaching, Scripture is encountered through the worship service or liturgy. It is the Word of God, read and preached and received, that calls the Christian community together to worship. Without Christian worship there would be no Bible. The Bible, in a very real sense, is the product of the early church's common prayer. Through worship, as the community of faith gathers, Scripture comes to life. Congregations that follow the Christian calendar and lectionary readings provide congregants with opportunities to participate in the story of God. The reading of Scripture is an interpretive act that provides an opportunity for worshippers to encounter the living Word of God.

It is ironic that some Evangelicals and Wesleyans who view Scripture as primary and authoritative for faith and practice do not practice regular reading of Scripture in worship. In order for Scripture to be formative in the life of the church, it must be read, experienced, and interpreted as a central aspect of the worshipping community. Also, through responsive readings, hymns, and choruses (assuming they have a biblical basis), the faith community provides various avenues for worshippers to interact with God's message through Scripture and thus be changed.

Congregations that participate in the Eucharist also encounter God through active expressions of Scripture in sacred ritual. The concept of the Word and Table or Word and Sacrament is drawn from a particular theology of worship that has its roots deep in the early church. A service of the Word and Table is worship that emphasizes the dual aspects of the spoken Word built around Scripture and the embodied Word centered on the celebration of the Eucharist or Communion. Once the proclaimed Word is preached, the congregants respond to the spoken Word by participation in the embodied Word of Communion.

For Wesley, the Eucharist was an opportunity to experience and commune with Christ. Through Communion persons experience the very presence of Christ. Wesley taught that Christ was present in the elements of Communion. His desire to see Christians take Communion regularly was based on both obedience to Christ and the hope that blessing and holiness would follow the use of this essential means of grace. The Eucharist, according to Wesley, served as a channel of grace that forms and transforms the believer. It is formative for those who are being drawn toward holiness and those who have been sanctified. For those desiring to grow in God's grace, which is a deepening of love for God and neighbor, Communion is the ordinary means of such growth. The sacrament serves not only to preserve and sustain but also to stimulate further growth in faith and holiness.

Questions to Ponder

1. How often do you actually do serious Bible reading? When you do, are you looking primarily for information relevant to your immediate need—a teaching lesson or a preaching assignment? Do you read the Bible primarily to determine what you are supposed to believe about something?

2. Do you accept the central point of this article? It is that the key reason for Bible reading is not to gather religious information, but to be *changed*, formed by God, to become *holy*.

3. We now live in an "information age." Is all the information in the Bible helpful for Christian life—including, for instance, practices of sacrifice explained in the Old Testament? Do some preachers and teachers use the Bible almost as a religious spreadsheet of doctrinal highlights and supposed systems of future prediction? Should they?

4. This article identifies several practical ways that one can approach Bible reading to encourage its formative potential. Which of them suggests to you the most practical way for stimulating your own growth in biblical holiness? Are you ready to focus seriously on its use in your own life?

5. Try to put in your own words how the "Table" (Communion) can function as a vital "means of grace" in your spiritual life.

Chapter 5

Holiness and Eccentricity: Finding a Workable Holiness Past

Douglas M. Strong

Focus: Holiness people often are thought of as older believers belonging to an earlier time. The stereotype runs as follows. There was little laughter in that time now long passed, partly because holiness people had so many prohibitions against most forms of entertainment. The numerous "don'ts" were a damper on a well-rounded life. Men were stern and dominant; women were complacent and dressed very modestly. There seemingly is little in this dour picture of a cramped spiritual life that would attract modern people to the faith. But is this a fair picture, and is there something from the holiness past, stereotype and all, that is worthy of guiding Christian believers in the twenty-first century? Can there be something attractive about being "eccentric," fools for Christ? Church historian Douglas Strong is confident that there is.

What meaning has the nineteenth-century Holiness Movement heritage for the broader understanding of the Wesleyan tradition? What does this heritage have to say to the pastoral concerns and challenges of our new millennium? What, if anything, is the "workable" past that can be gleaned from the nineteenth-century Holiness paradigm? To answer such questions, we first must come to terms with several substantive critiques of nineteenth-century Wesleyan thought. These interpretative judgments must be addressed squarely before there can be any affirming of the nineteenth-century paradigm and then any retrieval of nineteenth-century holiness themes for contemporary theology.

Three Critical Analyses

The three major critical analyses of nineteenth-century Wesleyanism have been: the Calvinist critique, the liberal critique, and the postliberal critique. I will explain each briefly.

1. The Calvinist Critique. The first critical evaluation—the Calvinist critique—was the theological challenge that American Methodism confronted from its very beginnings in North America. Since Calvinist forms of Christianity predominated within early American religion, Methodism was considered to be a theological intruder in relation to the dominant spirituality of the early Republic. Today's representatives of this critique interpret nineteenth-century American religious history primarily as the story of fanatical emotionalism, anti-intellectualism, and works righteousness. They agree that the nineteenth century was the "Methodist century," as some religious historians have called it, but they believe that this fact was exactly the problem with the nineteenth century.

Ironically, although Holiness churches were long resistant to cultural accommodation, they have now identified with the consumerism that typifies so many of today's American Christians. It seems that current Holiness churches have forgotten their nineteenth-century roots. Many of them have largely lost their distinctiveness—sometimes thriving numerically in the process, but without their saltiness. Some have read this change as the death of the true holiness movement. It is dead because, on the popular level, it has accepted the Calvinist critique in place of its own intended and "eccentric" identity.

2. The Liberal Critique. If the first critique of the Wesleyan/Holiness message in America came from the Calvinists in the early part of the nineteenth century, the second critique came later from the liberal, bourgeois wing of "Gilded Age" Methodism. Since Holiness advocates often came from socially marginalized contexts and exhibited ecstatic, Spirit-filled faith expressions, the rising middle class of Methodism disdained this enthusiastic reminder of their own unsophisticated frontier past.

By the twentieth century, most Methodist leaders viewed Holiness institutions as a relic of a bygone era. Soon (they hoped) they would fade away. Thus, many of the newly-gentrified, mainline Methodists dealt with the Holiness message and Holiness people by simply ignoring them. Mainline scholars in the first half of the twentieth century did not consider the older Wesleyan theological tradition as something that had any currency for the modern world. When Holiness people claimed that they were the ones who were consistent Wesleyans, their affirmations fell on deaf ears. Mainliners were not interested in who was being faithful to Wesley but who was most accepting of progressive theological trends.

3. The Post-liberal Critique. If the liberal contention is that Holiness advocates were not modern enough, then the post-liberal contention is that Holiness advocates were too "modern." As the third major group of nineteenth-century critics, the post-liberal critique has arisen relatively recently, in conjunction with more generalized negative appraisals of "modernity" (meaning Enlightenment rationalism). Among United Methodists, the post-liberal perspective has developed in combination with the late twentieth-century resurgence of Wesleyan studies which rediscovered John Wesley as a theological mentor. This rediscovery judged the nineteenth-century American expression of the Wesleyan message to be flawed by the modifications it made to the original Wesleyan message. They intended to leapfrog right over the nineteenth century and go directly back to the eighteenth—Wesley's time.

Many of these criticisms are directed at the compromises of mainline nineteenth-century Methodism, particularly the liberal emphasis on moral development rather than the traditional Wesleyan stress on the new creation in Christ. Because the Methodist church participated so uncritically in an accommodation to the emerging capitalist society, it became thoroughly "domesticated." In part, the agenda of the Holiness Movement in the nineteenth century was a response to these notorious aspects of mainline Methodism's capitulation to modernity. Holiness folks, for instance, condemned Methodism's neglect of marginalized people, as well as Methodism's acceptance of liberal theology.

Rising Above the Critiques

Despite the obvious inadequacies of the nineteenth-century Holiness Movement, pointed out fairly or unfairly by its many critics, I am still convinced that there are important lessons to be learned by studying this Holiness Movement. It is not essential that we throw out the Holiness baby with the bathwater of modernity. What is most intriguing to me about the nineteenth-century Holiness Movement is the way in which it was simultaneously both very modern and not very modern at all.

In fact, the claim that nineteenth-century folks were uncritically captured by modernity fails to comprehend the nuanced approach to modernity by Holiness people. Similarly, the typical liberal assertion that Holiness people were unsophisticated, unthinking backwoods people who failed to engage with the challenges of modernity misses the Holiness point altogether. The Holiness Movement displayed a more subtle interplay with its culture than is often recognized, accepting certain aspects of modernity while deftly excluding others.

Let us take as an example the early nineteenth-century tendency toward optimism. It is true that Wesleyans after the Civil War were optimists regarding the possibility of social reform. They truly believed that God's kingdom could come on earth—that the nation could be converted to Christ and that Christ's reign of justice could be effected soon. But before we dismiss this concept as naively quixotic, let us remember that it was precisely this conviction that motivated sanctified abolitionists to popularize the crusade against slavery. This also led many Wesleyans to champion women's rights, temperance, and other social reforms. They may not have ushered in the Kingdom, but they did help to move America toward a more just society.

But even while presenting the possibility of God's soon-arriving Kingdom, these holiness Wesleyans also were pessimistic about human nature, knowing the persistence of sin. They knew the difference between the optimism of grace and the optimism of culture. While mainline Methodists eventually transformed their religious optimism into a modernist notion of self-help and an unquestioning acceptance of American global expansionism, Holiness advocates began to have doubts about the inevitable progress of human society.

Although nineteenth-century Christians insisted on certain momentary spiritual events, the reality of religious life for Holiness people was a continual religious enthusiasm. The central factor for nineteenth-century Holiness people was the immediacy of the power of God This dynamic gospel message promoted connectedness with God and with one another. To know God was to be transformed, so that the vital, intimate relationship with Jesus modeled an intimate relationship with others. The faith life of Holiness men and women consisted of God's indwelling that was to lead to concrete ethical action.

Being Eccentric for Christ

While some Holiness disdain for modern values may have been a conservative resistance to change, for others it was much more. It was a radical refusal to accommodate the claims of the Christian gospel to the debilitating effects of consumerist culture that undermine faith in God and community with others by encouraging the sins of envy, greed, pride, and indulgence. Because we have been accepted by God, Holiness people declared, we thereby are called to accept others. The converts at the holiness camp meetings welcomed strangers in their midst—those left aside by the larger society. They were able to be so open-hearted because their spiritual union with Christ impelled them to move beyond themselves toward others.

Just as Christ does not exist merely for himself, but extends himself for the sake of human beings, so Christian believers are truly human when they move outside of their own self-centeredness. Theologically, this self-limiting vulnerability becomes evident in the life of Jesus. This counter-cultural kind of life is what was once called Christ's "eccentric" existence. It is to be mirrored in our own human "eccentricity," our being "fools" like and for Christ. Through our holy self-limitation, we are set free to love others. To be fully human, we must step outside the circle of ourselves in order to bring others into the larger circle of reconciliation. Eccentricity is the very nature of Christ, and thus, it should be so for us also.

The "sanctified eccentricity" of nineteenth-century Holiness people offers us a living tradition on which to draw, one that is particularly well-suited for today's world. We share with our friends from one hundred and fifty years ago a suspicion that modern assumptions have their limitations. We suspect that quality of life in today's world will no longer depend solely on the modern capacity to change structures or to produce more things to buy and sell.

As "post-moderns" who acknowledge continuity with our past, we can strip away the modern blinders that have prevented us from seeing clearly our need for genuine connectedness with God and one another. In so doing, we will be able to re-create the experiences of women and men who promoted the immediacy of God's presence for the sake of God's world—a sanctified eccentricity. It is in the recovery of this ethos that our nineteenth-century Holiness forebears can help us the most.

Questions to Ponder

1. First come the negative words: dour, stern, sad, straight-laced, excessively modest, anything but fun-loving, always restrained and against anything that might give the slightest appearance of evil. Are these mere stereotypes of old-time holiness people? Is this what it means to be Christ-like? Will such lives draw people to churches today?

2. Are you aware of the "liberal" critique of holiness, even if you have never thought of it in those words? Does a "holy" Christian belong in a religious museum filled with people who chose faith over edu-

cation and emotional fanaticism over reason and order? Are holy people always the marginalized of society, the unsophisticated people who reject high culture, resist change, and think nothing and do nothing that has not been thought and done before?

3. Douglas Strong suggests that the Holiness Movement of the nineteenth century was largely a critical response to Christians who were compromising their faith. They were yielding to the un-Christian values of American capitalism and ignoring the "poor" people being left behind. Should such a critical response be happening again today? Should people who worship a holy God reject the greed of the rich and minister with compassion to the poor?

4. Nineteenth-century holiness people are said to have held a wise and delicate balance of optimism and pessimism. They believed in the world-changing power of God's grace while remaining very aware of the depth of human sin. Has this balance been lost today? Do you think that today's world is beyond hope, or are there other options?

5. Holiness is said to be "women and men who promote the immediacy of God for the sake of God's world." Is this a clear and helpful definition of "holiness" for you?

PART 2

EXPERIENCE OF HOLINESS

Chapter 6

Holiness and Salvation:
Is There Hope for All People?

PHILIP R. MEADOWS

Focus: Has the Holy God made provision for the pursuit of holiness among people of non-Christian religions, a spiritual state acceptable to God? If so, does this gracious and universal provision include even those who never hear or confess the name of Jesus? We now live in a "pluralistic" world more than ever before. Multiple faith traditions are close neighbors, probably including wherever you live. Should Christians continue to insist that salvation is a possibility *only* through explicit faith in Jesus Christ?

What is the essence of true religion? A key concept in the theology of John Wesley is "prevenient grace," a divine enablement which the Holiness Movement has insisted is given to *all* sinful people. Philip Meadows suggests that this grace could make the exercise of faith and the pursuit of holiness possible—even from *inside* although not *because of* non-Christian traditions.

True religion for John Wesley consists in a heart set right toward God and neighbor. He speaks of true religion in terms of simplicity and purity. The Christian life is shaped by the singular intention to serve God and neighbor, a service flowing from a heart ordered by holy affections. A holy person, then, is one dispositionally and devotionally in tune with the divine will. In short, true religion is synonymous with holiness of heart and life, defined by holy love. Such love provides the inner power that enables all outward forms of the truly holy life.

Loving God with all our hearts and our neighbors as ourselves fulfills the law of Christ. True religion is "heart-religion," a religion of love. For Wesley, love is the life, the soul, and the spirit of religion as intended by God. True religion is to be identified with the kingdom of God that lies within; it is having heaven in the heart. Authentic salvation, the more excellent way, is about the pursuit of holiness before it is about going to heaven when we die. Any claim to authentic Christianity must be evaluated against this truth. What about all other religions?

True Religion and Christianity

True religion cannot be evaluated merely by the criteria of either right thinking or right doing, for the outward activities of both mind and life can belie the heart's true inward condition. Thus, in John Wesley's view, true religion can neither be reduced to *orthodoxy* (having the right system of beliefs or opinions), nor to *morality* or *honesty* (the outward practice of justice, mercy and truth), nor to *formality* (the attending to all the outward observances of religious practice without the inner reality). All of these characteristics belong to true religion and are conducive to it, but by themselves they still fall short of it. True religion, when it is "real" religion, refers to having the inward, substantial reality of a *transformed heart* that can give rise to the proper outward expressions of religious life.

Although Wesley typically equates religion and true Christianity, he makes the possibility of holy love and the possession of right tempers into a more inclusive principle. For instance, he concedes that many "ancient heathens" were taught of God, by God's inward voice, making it possible for them to pursue the essentials of true religion. So, Wesley appears to uphold the possibility of final salvation outside Christianity, based upon an authentically holy life. Even so, for him this possibility is never *without Christ*. He is careful to emphasize that this possibility is only through the universal operation of prevenient grace, which extends throughout the world to all human beings.

Wesley teaches us that the light of prevenient grace is a universal benefit of the meritorious death of Christ on the cross. Christ does not give light to the soul separate from, but in and with himself. There is a constant connection made between the *Son of God* and the *Spirit of Christ* present with us and at work in every human heart. This is typical of the way that Wesley identifies the work of grace and the presence of the Spirit as the universal possibility for salvation and holy living. No one is wholly void of the grace of God. Therefore, no one sins because there is no grace, but because they do not respond to the grace they have been given.

In light of this, we can find in Wesley's theology some patterns of thought that lead us toward an "inclusivist" approach to the theology of religions. At one level, this will mean facing the criticism of all inclusivist options, that of interpreting other religions through Christian categories and, therefore, denying their own truth claims on their own terms. This is certainly unavoidable for any theologian seeking to reconcile the particularity of truth revealed *through* Jesus Christ with the universal possibility of salvation *in* Jesus Christ.

Even so, salvation understood as the pursuit of holiness can provide us with a way of understanding and affirming the essentials of true religion among people of other religious traditions. serve as a larger category of religious reality than the theologies and practices of religion. Holiness pursued, with the help of God's prevenient grace, can include (rather than exclude) multiple ways of being "religious" as ways that are acceptable to God. This is a possibility that extends from the here to the hereafter.

Christianity and the World's Religions

I want to identify four principles that can inform the construction of a contemporary Wesleyan theology of religions. The principles will include both the universality and the particularity of God's saving work in Christ. I will, on the one hand, affirm the possibility that people of non-Christian religions may participate in the way of salvation and, on the other hand, ground that affirmation in Jesus Christ.

1. Reading True Religion Broadly. John Wesley did not discuss the saving potential of other ways of being religious in terms of their own beliefs and practices. This is not surprising since he had little experience with non-Christian peoples, and did not have access to the wealth of understanding now available to us through the study of religions. We are able today to see that many of the world's religious traditions (including Judaism, Islam, and Hinduism) would uphold the love of God and neighbor as a central religious principle. It seems reasonable to suggest, therefore, that we might extend Wesley's hints about the possibility of true religion among non-Christians.

The idea of sanctification (as the pursuit of holiness and salvation made possible by God's grace in Jesus Christ) can become the primary category for both including and evaluating the quality of all religious life. Love is the highest and most inclusive criterion of true religion. We might say that true religion consists in the transformation of hearts and lives, properly defined as "faith active in love," even if that faith is an "implicit" response to prevenient grace, the work of the Spirit of Christ.

2. Reading the World Providentially. With John Wesley, we can speak of one covenant of grace that includes God's presence and activity among different peoples and in different ways to achieve the divine plan of salvation for all creation. Such a stance entails an emphasis on creation and covenant that brings openness to the saving presence of the Spirit dispensed among non-Christian peoples. It is in this sense that other ways of being religious can be seen as having providential roles in God's plan of salvation for the world.

In the sermon "On Divine Providence," Wesley affirms the idea that God's providential love and care "includes the whole race of mankind, all the descendants of Adam, all the human creatures that are dispersed over the face of the earth." In its broadest sense, saving faith could be described as a responsive awakening of the heart through the operation of God's prevenient grace. It is God who enables all, in their own contexts, to be faithful in the pursuit of holiness, whatever the outward forms of faith and holy living.

Reading the world providentially can mean affirming: (1) that the saving presence and activity of God exist outside the Christian tradition; (2) that a saving response to God's grace can take different forms; (3) that different ways of being religious can act as means of prevenient grace through the responsive pursuit of holy living; (4) that those who respond in this way are accepted by God; and (5) that such acceptance is based on a response of faith to the Spirit of Christ, seen in the transformation of heart and life.

Wherever there is moral truth and right action, there is grace at work. Wherever there is love for God and neighbor, there is grace at work. Reading human beings graciously means affirming that all people are graced by the saving presence of the Spirit and capable of participating in God's providential purposes for the world. Rather than understanding this view as a threat to the uniqueness of Christianity, it could be seen as a cause for greater optimism that there is hope for faithful people in other religious traditions.

3. Reading Salvation in View of Christ. It is only through the particular truth of Jesus Christ that we can affirm the universal possibility of salvation and different ways of being religious as genuine means of God's grace. Human beings are oriented to the God of Jesus Christ through the Spirit of Christ who acts preveniently to shape the religious life of all people. Participating in the way of salvation, therefore, is not *because of* the religious beliefs and practices of any tradition (including Christianity). Rather, salvation is the transformation of hearts and lives by the Spirit of Christ. Any way of being religious that promotes this holiness transformation could be considered a means of God's prevenient grace and a participation in the way of salvation.

Different ways of being religious could have saving potential if they promote patterns of holy love that are Spirit inspired and Jesus shaped. The only criterion for holiness of heart and life that has been revealed to us is the person and work of Jesus. Insofar as any way of being religious can represent an instance of true religion, then we might say that it is the Spirit of Christ who enables Hindus to become Christ-like Hindus, Buddhists to become Christ-like Buddhists, and Muslims to become Christ-like Muslims.

4. Reading Mission Dialogically. God's providence and grace weave together to provide a basis for the common pursuit of holiness, social caring, and the struggle for justice. Christians, therefore, should enter into interreligious dialogue and cooperation. Doing so means responding to what God is doing in and through us and others. This openness to dialogue, however, does not detract from the task of evangelism, that is, inviting all people to embark on the more excellent way and to become followers of Jesus Christ. If salvation is Jesus shaped, and human flourishing is defined by Christ-likeness, then it certainly is appropriate to say that *fullness* of salvation can only be found through conscious and explicit faith in Christ.

God's prevenience and providence become a preparation for the proclamation of the gospel of Christ. They keep open the possibility that all people can be drawn to God, first through prevenient grace and then on to the fullness of grace in a fully conscious and saving relationship to Christ. It is the purpose of the Spirit of Christ to direct all people to the person of Christ, and it is the responsibility of Christians to seek to enable this to happen.

Questions to Ponder

1. Do you understand the concept of "prevenient grace"? How does it relate to believing that salvation is possible for all sinful people? See the "Orientation" to this chapter for a brief definition of this special kind of divine grace.

2. Is the presence and work of Jesus Christ essential for the potential salvation of people who never hear of him and thus never consciously accept him as their Lord? Can people become truly holy by gaining the "mind of Christ" without even knowing about Christ?

3. Holiness is said to be a religious category larger than theologies and religious practices approved by "orthodox" Christianity. If larger, then presumably it can be seen as reaching to all people. Do you agree with this? Does this endanger the special status of Christianity?

4. Can a Muslim become a Christ-like Muslim, a "sanctified" person acceptable to God although still a faithful Muslim? If so, what is the impact of this possibility on the Christian mission? If one can become Christ-like without knowing Jesus Christ, is it still important to share the full story of the Christ with all people?

Chapter 7

Holiness as a Second Blessing: More than Justification

TIMOTHY L. SMITH

Focus: When people are converted, the Bible describes them as being justified. Jesus Christ has become their "Savior." He is also their "Lord;" however, most new converts have not totally consecrated their lives to God until they have gone through a gradual process of sanctification. According to Timothy Smith, John Wesley held that Christian believers, subsequent to conversion, may experience a second blessing—a second work of divine grace in their lives, which empowers them to live Christ-like lives. Wesley further held that God helps to perfect believers' love toward God and others by their being entirely sanctified, that is, being wholly consecrated by the empowerment of God's Holy Spirit. This instantaneous work in the lives of believers aids them in becoming more and more like Christ.

John Wesley taught that Christians experienced gradual sanctification. But in the fall of 1739, he came to the clear conviction that a second and instantaneous experience was essential to that process. In that moment, believers were filled with the Holy Spirit; their hearts were cleansed from the remains of inbred sin, and they were perfected in love.

The assistance that a correct understanding of these events gives in the task of interpreting various aspects of Wesley's teaching and behavior now requires spelling out. I wish, first, to stress the light they shed on Wesley's own spiritual experience.

Wesley's Spiritual Experience

John Wesley himself acknowledged his disappointment at the small measure of joy he had received when he thought the Holy Spirit bore witness to his regeneration at the famous prayer meetings in Aldersgate Street, London, in May, 1738. He was tempted to doubt whether he had actually experienced what the Scripture promised. This fact has prompted some modern scholars to denigrate the Aldersgate event. It seems to me, rather, to have reflected the fact that Wesley at that point understood the Bible to teach only one instantaneous experience of saving grace and that, therefore, all the promises of Scripture concerning the righteousness, peace, and joy that were to flow from the presence and work of the Holy Spirit should have been evident immediately after he was assured of being God's child. On the contrary, he found himself a few days afterward nearly "sawn asunder" by doubt, temptation, and the absence of joy.

What Wesley soon learned was that the Moravians believed that the witness of the Spirit to regeneration was usually bestowed sometime after one was forgiven and enabled to have victory over sinning. In his letter of October 30, 1738, to his brother Samuel, he equated that witness with "'the seal of the Spirit,' 'the love of God shed abroad in my heart,' and . . . 'joy in the Holy Ghost,' joy which 'no man taketh away,' 'joy unspeakable and full of glory.' " Such a degree of faith, he wrote to Samuel from Germany, "purifies the heart" and "renews the life after the image of our blessed Redeemer." Here was the germ of what became a year later his doctrine of entire sanctification. But at this point, Wesley was still thinking only of degrees of saving faith.

Holiness and Expectations

During the months which followed that trip to Germany, and particularly after Wesley joined Whitefield in leading the awakening in Bristol and London in the spring and summer of 1739, Wesley carefully studied the Scriptures concerning "babes in Christ" and the degrees of faith. They confirmed his belief that those who, under his and his brother's ministry as well as that of Whitefield, had professed to have been instantaneously transformed by the Holy Spirit from "the faith of a servant," as he put it, to "the faith of a child of God" were undoubtedly born again.

Now, in the fall of 1739, Wesley became convinced that Scripture taught that this fullness would accompany a second and deeper moment of hallowing grace, which would bring also purity of heart and perfect love. He turned then from bemoaning the incompleteness of his peace and joy in regeneration to marveling at the measure of grace that he and his converts had received, and at the fullness that was to come. Now, hungering and thirsting after righteousness became a joyful experience. He was confident that entire sanctification, or purity from the remains of inward corruption, would also guarantee his final perseverance and so make his satisfaction complete.

Eventually, Wesley's followers who sought and found this blessing taught him that he still expected too much; and his study of the experience of Jesus and the apostles confirmed that he had. Hence, in 1765, when he republished the preface to the hymnbook of 1740 in his *Plain Account of Christian Perfection*, Wesley inserted several footnotes to show where he had overstated the subjective fruits of full salvation. He explained how the fall from grace of several notable Methodists, whom he could not doubt had once enjoyed perfect love, had convinced him in the late 1750s that this experience assured only present, not final salvation. But from 1740 onward, Wesley never questioned the idea of an instant of heart cleansing in a second moment of sanctifying grace.

Scripture and Experience

We may safely conclude, then, that the doctrine of perfect love emerged both from scriptural study and from the certainty Wesley felt about the genuineness of the faith of his converts. Holiness of heart seemed to him, as it has ever since to his followers, what every person who is truly saved by faith will long for. He was convinced that this "great salvation from sin" would be sent down, as at the day of Pentecost unto "all generations, into the hearts of all true believers," and that the promise was "to all them that are afar off, even as many as the Lord shall call."

Wesley also believed that real Christians would grow in holiness both before they received the blessing of sanctifying faith and afterwards, not by works of righteousness but by the grace of God. This the Holy Spirit brought to them both by the inspiration of His presence and by the "means of grace" — prayer, thanksgiving, obedience, self-denial, studying the Scriptures, and faithful attendance on preaching and upon the sacrament of holy communion.

Holiness and "Enthusiasm"

Those who had long opposed Wesley and Whitefield as "enthusiasts" for teaching the actual presence and work of the Holy Spirit in the lives of Christian believers rushed to publicize the disagreements between the two evangelists. They seized upon Wesley's new doctrine of heart purity as proof of their charge. The extent of the pressure is evident from the fact that some of Wesley's closest followers drew back.

Apparently in 1745, Wesley decided that preaching Christian perfection to persons not yet converted was neither scriptural nor practical. He began to rely instead upon bands and "select societies," to which he assigned persons who were clearly in the experience of regeneration and clearly seekers or finders of full salvation. If the Minutes of the First Conference of 1745 actually reflect his practice, for the next dozen years Wesley confined his own preaching of the details of the second experience to those who had found the first.

Centrality of Holiness

In pursuing this strategy, however, the Wesleys and their preachers developed great skill in inserting the doctrine of Christian holiness into every treatise, without defining it in great detail. When we understand and believe what the evidence tells us about the maturing of John's convictions on the subject in 1739 and 1740, his seemingly innocuous phrases that couple justification with heart purity in many different ways appear in their true light. Wesley became increasingly confident that to declare that the God of love had given His children the two "great commandments" was to assure them that they might also receive by faith, through the Holy Spirit, that holiness of heart that was required to obey them.

In his published writings, therefore, Wesley for many years emphasized progressive sanctification more than the moment of the Holy Spirit's cleansing, though he never failed to use language that enabled his followers to understand that he was contending for both the gradual and the instantaneous work of God's Spirit. In more private documents, however, as for example in the unpublished Conference Minutes of 1744 and 1747, in his correspondence not intended for publication, and in essays and correspondence circulated privately, he carefully explained the second moment of grace.

Holiness and Pentecost

Wesley's use of Pentecostal language came to a climax in his *Farther Appeal to Men of Reason and Religion,* published in 1745. There he set forth at length the teaching of the Scriptures, the Church of England, and the post-apostolic fathers on the work of the Holy Spirit in bringing to believers both the assurance of salvation and the experience of sanctification. In response to published criticism of his earlier statements about the baptism or fullness of the Spirit, Wesley emphasized the following:

> Christians now "receive," yea, are "filled with the Holy Ghost," in order to be filled with the fruits of that blessed Spirit. And he inspires into all true believers now, a degree of the same peace and joy and love which the apostles felt in themselves on that day when they were first "filled with the Holy Ghost."

Wesley stressed during the same period, however, the work and gift of the hallowing Spirit, as distinct from His fullness, in the experience of regeneration. His most persuasive passages on this subject appeared in the same *Farther Appeal*. But of equal doctrinal significance are the sermons on regeneration that he preached between 1739 and 1745. These sermons, as well as his letters and the volumes of his Journal composed in those years constantly, allude to the love of God being "shed abroad" in the hearts of persons born again, and to the process of sanctification that accompanied their quest for the experience of perfect love.

Wesley's Theology of Love

So Wesley almost eliminated his use of the dramatic phrase "baptism with the Holy Ghost," preferring instead the one the Apostles are recorded as having used after Pentecost, that is, "filled" with the Spirit. Even for this one he preferred such synonymous phrases as "filled with love," or "filled with all the fullness of God." These focused the hearer's attention upon what Wesley thought most important, and most endangered: the ethical meaning of the righteousness which must exceed that of scribes and Pharisees, of the perfection in love that flows from the faith that God's love, or faithfulness, inspires.

Of course, for trinitarian Christians to suggest that the Holy Spirit is not the One who first communicates divine love to believers and who thereafter presides over its progress and perfection in hallowing their hearts was and is, to say the least, a theological oddity. Hence, Wesley always taught *both* regeneration *and* entire sanctification in a Pentecostal frame of reference. But in doing so he had to cope with popular misconceptions of it and with the spread of antinomianism among his evangelical associates.

Using these and other similar terms, moreover, contributed directly to Wesley's overall objective — to preach righteousness, to help believers and himself and his brother Charles to keep foremost that "holiness without which no man shall see God." He understood such holiness to reflect the character he ascribed to the Lord of both the Old and the New Testaments — a God of ethical love, expressed in faithfulness to lost humanity and especially to the poor and oppressed.

When that love triumphed over all its enemies in our fallen natures, the result he usually called purity of heart, salvation from sin, Christian perfection, or full restoration to the image of God. His teaching of such a second blessing, his preaching of what was in fact Pentecostal holiness, was indeed the apogee of John Wesley's theology of love.

Plain Account of Christian Perfection

Finally, Wesley issued his *Plain Account of Christian Perfection* in 1765, gathering together materials both recent and well-nigh forgotten that he had published during the preceding twenty-five years. He wrote it to counter the charge that the emphasis upon an instantaneous experience of perfect love was a new departure for him. Wesley declared instead what I have concluded was factually correct, that he and his brother had taught this doctrine consistently since the publication of the preface to the hymnbook of 1740.

The task of all true Wesleyans, I think, is to promote that purity of heart and perfect love that flow from "the fullness of Him that filleth all in all." In the face of the present questions, I think Wesley would ask ones like these. If we truly love God, ought we not to love Him with all our hearts, and other persons as ourselves? And are not God's commands implied promises that we will be enabled to keep them? God's promise to cleanse you "from all your filthiness and all your idols," to put His Spirit within you and cause you to keep His commandments, is, Wesley would say, one of a chain of biblical promises that call us to perfect love.

Questions to Ponder

1. In what way may growth in Christ-likeness be gradual, and in what way may growth be instantaneous?

2. How may our expectations about holiness help or hinder us with regard to growth in Christ-likeness?

3. Although Wesley based his beliefs primarily on the Bible, to what degree may it be confirmed (or disconfirmed) by our experiences?

4. Is salvation only a matter of conversion, of regeneration? In what way is salvation also a matter of sanctification, of growth in love toward God and others?

5. How may small accountability groups—what Wesley called "bands" or "select societies"—provide the best context for growth in holiness?

Chapter 8

Holiness and Discipleship: Saved to Serve

ALLAN COPPEDGE

Focus: People become holy through the redemption of Jesus Christ. It occurs by grace through faith. After conversion, God views people as holy because of the righteousness of Christ. God also wants them to become holy—to become like Christ. According to Allan Coppedge, this process occurs by God's grace; it also occurs through discipleship. Becoming disciples of Christ, especially in the context of small discipleship groups, contributes to a Christian's progressive sanctification, becoming entirely sanctified by grace. Entire sanctification promotes love and service to God, which in turn promotes love and service to others. Such love and service are aided by spiritual disciplines that fulfill the Great Commission as well as holy living.

Wesleyan theology has made a distinct contribution to understanding Christian holiness in three areas: (1) Holiness as an over-arching theme in scriptural truth; (2) Holiness as containing a crisis point in Christian experience called entire sanctification; and (3) Holiness of heart worked out in holiness of life by means of spiritual disciplines. Because the second of these, the experience of entire sanctification, has been the point most often neglected by both Wesleyans and non-Wesleyans alike, there has been a tendency to focus a great deal of energy and resources on the articulation and propagation of this central truth.

At the same time, faithfulness to Scripture and to our special theological heritage makes us conscious that this distinctive emphasis on entire sanctification can never be divorced from the context of the other two major contributions that Wesleyan theology has made. If or when this should happen, a grave disservice will have been done to the cause of truth and the holiness tradition, for it would isolate the experience of entire sanctification from its larger scriptural framework and fail to see that its full implications are worked out in godly living. I write for the purpose of preventing any such isolation of one part of our theological heritage from the rest.

Holiness and the People of God

The concept of holiness as an over-arching theme in Scripture begins with the character of the God of Scripture: He is the ultimate Holy One. Perhaps the clearest revelation of the centrality of God's holiness comes in the visions of Isaiah (Isa. 6) and John (Rev. 4), where both prophet from the Old Testament and apostle from the New Testament are permitted to see into the eternal world and hear the heavenly creatures declare the glory of God. But not only is God the Father styled in the Bible as holy, but the Son and the Spirit are as well.

If the holiness of Scripture begins with the character of God, it moves quickly to the question of the holiness of people. This is inferred from the data regarding the nature of God Himself: if He is holy, and He made people like Himself, it follows that in some sense people were designed to be holy as well. To be sure, it is a derived holiness, for only God is originally holy, but it is nevertheless holiness like the holiness of God.

But people are not holy! They have fallen into sin and disobedience, and rebellion has become characteristic of their lives. In spite of the universality of this unholiness (Rom. 5:12ff.), God still desires for people to be like Himself, and in His grace He has designed a scheme of redemption to make people holy again and restore them to fellowship with Himself.

From God's perspective holiness is not an optional extra for those who are members of the people of God. He is looking for a people who are holy as He is holy. He began making that clear with the establishment of the Old Covenant and continues to make His desires known under the New. His reason for wanting the same kind of people has not changed: "As he who called you is holy, be holy yourselves in all your conduct; since it is written, 'You shall be holy, for I am holy' " (1 Pet. 1:15–16).

The Process of Discipleship

The process of being like Jesus began for the twelve disciples with their conversion or with what is otherwise called initial sanctification. But the character of the twelve was not immediately like that of their Master. Character building is a process, and so Jesus, knowing this, invested three years of His life in developing the character of these disciples. This involved growth in grace that is sometimes designated as progressive sanctification, that is, that development of character under the authority of Jesus in the company of others of like commitment.

Another factor closely interwoven in the fabric of spiritual growth was the group of spiritual disciplines that Jesus began to build into His people from the very earliest days. Some of these have to be inferred from the data, like the importance of knowledge and truth, and thus the necessity of the study of the Word of God the importance of growing with other disciples, and thus the significance of being a regular part of a small fellowship of like-minded people.

In spite of the disciplined life that the twelve disciples developed and the investment of Jesus in them over a three-year period, they still lacked something in their own character when it was time for Him to leave them. Jesus was fully aware of this. That is why He spent the largest part of His last evening with them explaining the coming of the Holy Spirit and the implications for their lives. Then He closed with a prayer for their sanctification. Both the fulfillment of His teaching and the answer to His prayer came on the day of Pentecost when the disciples were filled with the Holy Spirit.

Holiness and the Great Commission

With this introduction to the process of making disciples, we turn to some of the specifics that relate holiness and discipleship. Jesus' next-to-the-last commandment is given in Matthew 28, and is commonly styled the Great Commission. Here Jesus is clearly speaking to believing disciples. There is no question about their being the redeemed people of God.

They also were people who are living under the authority of Jesus. They went to the mountain in Galilee in response to a commandment of the risen Christ when He first appeared in Jerusalem. Having met Him in obedience, they are further reminded by Jesus of the authority that He has from the Father. "All authority in heaven and on earth has been given unto me," is His preface to the Great Commission. If we too are submitting ourselves to His authority, it will be very difficult to escape the conclusion that we also have been commissioned to make disciples of all nations.

The Significance of Entire Sanctification for Discipleship

The role of entire sanctification or the baptism of the Holy Spirit for discipleship is significant in three major areas. One of these refers to what the disciples were and relates to the question of being or character. Another relates to the work that Jesus had called them to do. This is the matter of ministry or service. The third area is a connectional area between what they were to be and what they were to do.

The first area in which entire sanctification is significant for the concept of discipleship relates to the fact that, after Pentecost, God was is still looking for holy people. This brings us once again to the matter of character. Believers cannot be a holy people without being like the Father and the Son. The experience of entire sanctification is a part of that process. It seems to make its impact felt in at least four ways. (1) Entire sanctification places our will under the full control of the Holy Spirit, with the result that God can work out His perfectly holy character in our lives. (2) Entire sanctification also affects the character of disciples relative to their willingness to grow. (3) With entire sanctification a power from the Holy Spirit is available for a more disciplined life. (4) With the fullness of the Holy Spirit comes a power for victorious Christian living.

The second major area in which sanctification is significant for discipleship relates to the question of authority. It touches both the character of disciples—what they are, and their ministry—and what they do. The meeting place between authority and holiness in this context relates to the conditions of entire sanctification that are the same as those for a disciple who is living under the absolute, kingly rule of God.

The third major area in which sanctification makes its impact on the life of discipleship has to do with the ministry to which disciples are called. This includes, at least, three things. (1) Discipleship relates to the power from the Holy Spirit to be witnesses to Jesus in Jerusalem and in Judea and Samaria and to the uttermost part of the earth. (2) To make godly disciples people must be godly disciples. (3) With entire sanctification, the Holy Spirit has total control in the life of disciples over their spiritual gifts, other God-given abilities, time resources, and energy for the work and ministry.

The Significance of Discipleship for Sanctified Living

The effects of discipleship on the individual who has experienced entire sanctification are primarily twofold. The first is that it makes it possible to maintain the experience of sanctifying grace. There is no unconditional eternal security for the entirely sanctified any more than for the justified. Disciples have not only the model and teaching of Jesus to assist them, but the spiritual disciplines that are necessary for keeping life under the full control of God's sanctifying Spirit. These disciplines (for example, daily time in searching the Scripture and private prayer) are learned to help the disciple know God and obey His will.

Another aspect of discipleship that assists in the maintaining of the experience of entire sanctification is the regular fellowship with others committed to holy living. This consistent fellowship with other disciples provides a place for accountability in one's spiritual life so that means regular attention will be given to spiritual examination.

The Means of Making Disciples

When Jesus set out to create a holy people, that is, to make disciples, how did He go about it? What were His tools for building godly people? The first thing He did was invest His own life in them. This was one of the purposes of the incarnation, to demonstrate the process of making disciples after the likeness and character of a holy God. What Jesus did in the discipleship process ought to become a pattern for all who have been given the commission to make disciples in all nations.

This life-to-life investment included four elements. (1) Jesus became a model of the kind of godly life the Father wants to see in every Christian. (2) He invested Himself in His disciples by teaching them knowledge of the truth. (3) He was then a model and a teacher of the truth in His training of the twelve disciples, but also one who supervised the building into their priorities of the disciplines necessary to cultivate their relationship with God and make it possible for Him to work out His will in their lives and ministries. (4) Whereas the first three elements of Jesus' investment in His people relate primarily to their edification, the fourth pertains principally to equipping them for the work of ministry—for fulfilling the Great Commission.

Yet, after Jesus had spent three years of His life giving of Himself to His disciples, He knew there was still something missing in their lives. So, while Jesus' investment of Himself was the first part of making disciples, there was also a second major factor in His plan, namely, the baptism of the Holy Spirit.

Conclusion

Is it possible that our strong emphasis on the experience of the fullness of the Holy Spirit has led us to conclude (perhaps even subconsciously) that the Holy Spirit does everything in the life of a believer that Jesus does? With regard to the immediate relation with the Godhead, He does play an irreplaceable role. But, with regard to the discipleship process, can the Spirit play the same role as Jesus did in the flesh?

I submit that the Holy Spirit does not replace Jesus in this way. Jesus knew this very well. That is why He told His apostles that their job was to make disciples: They were to do in others' lives by their physical presence what He had done in theirs. It was a deliberate part of Jesus' plan to fulfill the Great Commission that those who were already disciples should invest themselves in others under His authority and through the power of His Spirit. Must not this life-to-life investment also become a crucial complement to our proclamation of sanctifying grace if we are to fully implement Jesus' strategy for making disciples of all nations?

Questions to Ponder

1. What do you consider the most helpful ways to undertake Christian discipleship?

2. How essential are small groups and the accountability that occurs among group members for Christian discipleship? What small group practices have you found to be most helpful?

3. What were (and are) Jesus' overarching concerns in charging his disciples in Matthew 28:19–20 with the "Great Commission"?

4. What is your understanding of entire sanctification? How does entire sanctification help Christians grow spiritually?

5. Which of the spiritual disciplines do you find most helpful?

Chapter 9

Holiness and Spiritualities: A Range of Christian Experience

DON THORSEN

Focus: Don Thorsen explores the variety of Christian spiritualities that have arisen in church history. Each tradition offers valuable insights that contribute to growth in faith, hope, and love. Thorsen considers the Wesleyan traditions of Christianity to be inclusive of other spiritualities, learning from them in order to enhance their own growth in holiness. The inclusive character of the Wesley, Methodist, and Holiness traditions encourages greater effort in cooperation and unity among Christians—effort known as "ecumenism." Learning from the variety of Christian spiritualities aids in holy living. It also aids Christians and churches to relate in ways that are complementary with one another, aiding them in living Christ-like lives and cooperating with one another in ministry.

For the past decade, I have been teaching a variety of courses in Christian spirituality. Mostly, I teach two courses in the Doctor of Ministry program at Azusa Pacific University. They are entitled "History of Christian Spirituality" and "Theology for Spiritual Formation." Although I am a trained theologian, I enjoy researching Christian spirituality inside and outside the Wesleyan, Methodist, and Holiness traditions. I also enjoy teaching about Christian spirituality to Doctor of Ministry students. They come from practically every tradition of Christianity. They are Protestant and Roman Catholic, mainline and evangelical, charismatic and non-charismatic, and so on.

In researching Christian spirituality, one of the more interesting discoveries I have made is the widespread recognition and appreciation of John Wesley. He is regularly viewed as a Protestant champion of what could be called, broadly speaking, the Holiness tradition of Christian spirituality. It is refreshing as well as interesting to see Wesley viewed so prominently in ecumenical publications.

The consideration of spirituality as a means for encouraging ecumenical dialogue is not a new idea. Such dialogues have gone on for quite a while in interdenominational ecumenism. However, Christians from the Wesleyan traditions, particularly the holiness branches, have not always realized the opportunities they have for participating in and contributing to present-day ecumenism. The surprising affirmation of the historic holiness spirituality and theology by ecumenically oriented Christians outside our holiness background encourages me. It encourages me with regard to the potential role the Wesleyan traditions have in contributing to Christian unity and cooperation.

Although the Wesleyan and Holiness tradition of spirituality is often categorized as just one form of Christian spirituality among many, its view of holiness as an expression of Christ-likeness aids ecumenical understanding and cooperation because of its inclusive nature and embrace of the varieties of Christian spirituality. I want to develop the ecumenical value of holiness by looking at its inclusive nature, which is embedded, albeit sometimes overlooked, in Wesleyanism. In particular, I want to investigate a Wesleyan understanding of holiness as it relates—in a complementary fashion—to the varieties of Christian spirituality.

Wesley and Ecumenism

Although John Wesley was a champion of holiness spirituality, it is a matter of debate as to whether or not he was a champion of ecumenism. Of course, we cannot finally determine Wesley's ecumenical acumen since he lived prior to the emergence of the 20th-century ecumenical movement. However, that has not prevented people from speculating. On the one hand, Wesley's emphasis on a "catholic spirit" has inspired innumerable Wesleyan and Methodist Christians to advocate ecumenism. For example, in his sermon entitled "Catholic Spirit," Wesley said:

> But although a difference in opinions or modes of worship may prevent an entire external union, yet need it prevent our union in affection? Though we can't think alike, may we not love alike? May we not be of one heart, though we are not of one opinion? Without all doubt we may. Herein all the children of God may unite, notwithstanding these smaller differences. These remaining as they are, they may forward one another in love and in good works.

On the other hand, Wesley expressed strong opinions about different views of theology and ministry, which sometimes left him in heated debate with church friends and foes. Wesley was well known for his debates with George Whitefield and Calvinists over predestination, with Bishop Lavington over enthusiasm, with Bishop Warburton over ecclesiastical boundaries, and so on. Wesley often agreed to disagree with other Christians. Yet, he remained charitable toward them, for example, in his enduring friendship with Whitefield. In sum, Wesley advocated and lived a catholic spirit that continues to influence Christians on behalf of greater unity and cooperation.

Wesley and Holiness

Although we may question Wesley's advocacy of ecumenism, we cannot question his advocacy of holiness. He clearly promoted "holiness of heart and mind." In *A Plain Account of Christian Perfection*, his premiere statement on Christian holiness and spirituality, Wesley said:

> Hence I saw, in a clearer and clearer light, the indispensable necessity of having "the mind which was in Christ," and of "walking as Christ also walked;" even of having, not some part only, but all the mind which was in Him; and of walking as He walked, not only in many or in most respects, but in all things.

The theme of holiness, especially when articulated as love, runs throughout Wesley's preaching and writing. In describing a true Christian, Wesley said that such a "one loves the Lord his God with all his heart, with all his soul, with all his mind, and with all his strength. . . . And loving God, he 'loves his neighbor as himself'."

Wesley's focus on holiness was expressed in a variety of ways. In addition to speaking about holiness in terms of love for God and neighbor, he also spoke of holiness in terms of joy, happiness, thankfulness, prayer without ceasing, purity, obedience, fruits of the Spirit, and doing all to the glory of God. As such, holiness represented both a gift and task. As a gift, God imputes righteousness to believers by God's saving grace through the work of Jesus Christ. As a task, God enlists those same believers to respond in faith, hope, and love to God's offer of sanctifying grace. God wants to impart righteousness to believers, as they become fellow workers with God in becoming more like Jesus Christ. In all instances, God initiates, nourishes, and completes the sanctifying process. Yet, God paradoxically requires our response to divine grace.

In this life, Wesley thought that believers might and should seek to experience "Christian perfection," a technical term used by Wesley, sometimes known as entire sanctification and other words used to express a mature Christian life. Sometimes conceived as a second work of grace subsequent to conversion, Wesley thought Christians should live a more holy life, enabled by the sanctifying work of the Holy Spirit in their lives. Such a life should manifest holy thoughts, words, and actions. Wesley was, in fact, optimistic with regard to how much the sovereign God of the universe might transform believers into holy examples of Christ-like living.

From our contemporary perspective, we might want to think of Wesley's concept of holiness as wholeness. The holistic pursuit of personhood represents the kind of holy healing Wesley thought that God wants to perform in our lives. Randy Maddox focuses on this idea in talking about the therapeutic nature of Wesley's understanding of salvation. He says: "This need (for healing) accounts for the prominence of therapeutic language (resonating with early Greek practice) in Wesley's various comments on human salvation. Indeed, Wesley characterized the very essence of religion as a *therapeia*—therapy by which the Great Physician heals our sin diseased souls, restoring the vitality of life that God intended for us."

Wesley represents a clear example among Protestants of one who promoted holiness in believers. He thought that greater holiness could occur among groups of believers and, indeed, in society as a whole. Just as Wesley was optimistic with regard to God's grace to perfect believers individually, he was optimistic with regard to how God could transform society. Many Christians inside and outside of Methodism have looked to Wesley for an example of a holistic as well as transformative understanding of Christian holiness.

Wesley and the Variety of Christian Spiritualities

A survey of contemporary literature on the subject of Christian spirituality reveals Wesley's prominence. In summary of such literature, let me list some of the typologies used by scholars to discuss Christian spirituality. For example, Richard Foster, who is Quaker, is a prominent, contemporary authority in Christian spirituality. In his book *Streams of Living Water*, he outlines what he considers to be six "great Traditions—streams of spiritual life if you will—and to note significant figures in each." They are:

The Contemplative Tradition, or the prayer-filled life;
The Holiness Tradition, or the virtuous life;
The Charismatic Tradition, or the Spirit-empowered life;
The Social Justice Tradition, or the compassionate life;
The Evangelical Tradition, or the Word-centered life;
The Incarnational Tradition, or the sacramental life.

In Foster's book as well as in other writings on the Christian life, Wesley figures prominently as a representative of holiness spirituality. Other typologies list a larger number of Christian spiritualities. Ben Campbell Johnson, a Presbyterian, lists seven types of spirituality. He lists Wesley, for example, as having an Ascetic Spirituality rather than a Holiness Spirituality per se, but the essence of the type remains the same. Gary Thomas, a Baptist, draws upon Carl Jung and Myers-Briggs "types" in identifying nine "spiritual temperaments," what he calls "sacred pathways":

(1) Naturalist, (2) Sensate, (3) Traditionalist, (4) Ascetic, (5) Activist, (6) Caregiver, (7) Enthusiast, (8) Contemplative, and (9) Intellectual.

In this typology, Wesley and the holiness tradition appear several places, as both Ascetics and Activists. While these typologies may not appeal to everyone in the holiness tradition, they reflect recognition of Wesley and the larger holiness embodiment of Christian spirituality. Most comprehensive studies of spirituality resist typologies and list a wide variety of Christian spiritualities, spanning the entirety of church history. It would not take long perusing The Westminster Dictionary of Christian Spirituality to find literally dozens of distinctive Christian spiritualities. Finally, in all these studies, Wesley remains a prominent and well respected leader—a crucial piece of the mosaic we call Christian spirituality.

Holiness, Inclusivity, and Exclusivity

I like to think of holiness as a holistic, inclusive form of Christian spirituality. Ideally, I think it is. Why? Holiness implies wholeness and completeness. In the Bible, God is referred to as being holy: "Holy, holy, holy is the Lord of hosts; the whole earth is full of his glory" (Isaiah 6:3, NRSV; cf. Revelation 4:8). Some consider the holiness of God as being representative of all God's perfections, all of God's transcendent characteristics. In Scripture, Christians are repeatedly called to live lives of holiness. In the Old Testament, Leviticus 11:44 says, "For I am the Lord your God; sanctify yourselves therefore, and be holy, for I am holy." In the New Testament, 1 Peter 1:15 says, "Instead, as he who called you is holy, be holy yourselves in all your conduct." In the Sermon on the Mount, Jesus makes the most profound call to holiness when he says, "Be perfect as your heavenly Father is perfect" (Matthew 5:48).

This call is to wholeness and completeness in every respect, as well as to a moral conception of godliness, usually thought to be representative of holiness spirituality. When holiness is viewed in relationship to the varieties of Christian spirituality, there is no reason to consider them in competition. On the contrary, it is not a matter of either holiness or some other form of spirituality, whether it is evangelical, sacramental, contemplative, activist, or charismatic. Holiness may be understood in essence as embracing all of the traditions of spirituality. It is a both/and relationship rather than one that is either/or. In fact, one could say that holiness, in the essential sense of the term, could be understood as a catchword that integrates all types of spirituality, just as holiness is used as an all-inclusive reference to the attributes of God.

Proponents of holiness must remain humble; other traditions have equal rights in expressing their views of spirituality, especially in claims to holism reflected in their spirituality. Proponents of holiness must also remain open—genuinely open—to learning from other Christian traditions of spirituality. Wesley arguably remained open to learning from others when his views were demonstrated to be deficient or wrong. Likewise, those of us in the holiness tradition need to be humble, yet bold in uplifting the ecumenical value of holiness.

Conclusion

John Wesley's focus on holiness continues to be an inspiration for contemporary Christian faith and practice. It is an inspiration for those of us in the holiness tradition who value holiness as an important descriptor of Christian spirituality, manifested in the transformation of individuals as well as the church and society.

Holiness is an inspiration for those who view Christian spirituality as a complex of valid expressions, and who consider holiness an integral component in understanding and affirming all Christians. It is an inspiration for those who seek ways of promoting ecumenical activities, realizing that a renewed focus on holiness may positively influence those inside the holiness tradition as well as those outside the tradition—those who want to enlist the value of holiness for the sake of greater unity and cooperation among Christians.

Questions to Ponder

1. In what ways may biblical holiness serve as a means for cooperation and unity among Christians?

2. How does the concept of holiness as "therapy" help us understand how God wants to heal as well as transform believers into greater Christ-likeness?

3. In studying the variety of Christian spiritualities, does it help to know that there is more than one way for believers to understand what it means to be spiritual? to be holy?

4. Although Christians may be drawn to a few particular ways of being spiritual, would it benefit them to explore alternative practices in order to aid their growth in holiness?

5. When Gary Thomas described nine "sacred pathways," with which one (or two) do you identify? How may this identification help you to grow more spiritually?

PART 3

APPLICATIONS OF HOLINESS

Chapter 10

Holiness and Relevance: Facing Difficult Social Issues

HAROLD B. KUHN

Focus: The people of God must make practical decisions about how to live in this troubled world. These decisions should reflect the holy love that now resides in them, and it should dare to address the painful social issues of our time. Being "holy" certainly does not mean that one suddenly has all the answers, particularly to complex social circumstances. However, holiness should heighten one's sensitivity to social evils and make bold one's determination to live in a prophetic way that is pleasing to God. In an earlier chapter by Douglas Strong, the point is made that holiness people of the nineteenth century resisted the obvious evils of society. They had an "optimism of grace" that encouraged their prophetic engagement with the evils of their time. Now Harold Kuhn extends the call to such social relevance. This is God's world. Surely, those who by grace share in the divine holiness are to love God's world and care for it and its people in all ways possible.

The biblical call to personal sanctity is one that places before us an obligation to embody in practical living the implications of the emphasis on Christian holiness. All experienced holiness is to be evident in the conduct of the Christian believer. The fine values which have historically marked the lives of the best of the saints are of little value as museum pieces; only as they find expression in the activities of our common life are they significant. The life which is pleasing to God issues from an inner spiritual state in which doubleness of purpose and chaos of motivation have been set at rest. The sanctified life is one which springs from a heart free "to will with God one will."

Beyond Negative Mandates

Divine revelation informs us that the Good and the Right are grounded, not merely in the structures of the cosmos, but in the will of a holy and sovereign God. It is none other than God who, grasping completely our needy and limited human predicament, has taken the initiative in disclosing the major lines and the central drive of the divine will. Even with this revelation, however, particulars can be troubling, and at times the Holiness Movement has made premature and faulty judgments.

It requires little historical knowledge to help us recall that offering the "easy answer" on occasion has tempted the ethical thinker within the Holiness Movement. This temptation was frequently implemented by the condemnation of certain actions which, in fact, turned out to be morally neutral and innocent in themselves. For example, the use of musical instruments was said to lead to two snares for Christian persons. Outside the church, they were inseparably connected with the social dance that nearly all sensitive Christians regarded as an evil. Within the church, the simple question of the choice of an organist frequently led to dissension within the body of believers. The rather natural defensive reaction was to challenge the use of any musical instruments in the church, in some cases to ban their use entirely, and in some cases to extend the prohibition to the homes of Christians.

Honesty demands that we recognize something. At times the Holiness Movement has tended to be little more than a conservative reaction to social and technological change. Each new social form and major new invention has tended to set off a rash of negative mandates for sensitive Christians. The usual history of those holiness people who reacted to new inventions in terms of "never" or "no child of mine" has been that later they became less vehement in their position, finally became muted in their opposition, and eventually adopted the new device in question. There is a lesson to be learned here.

Burning Issues of Our Time

It is time to note some of the living issues that confront the one who will embody the life of sanctity in our time. Realism demands that the life devoted to godliness be lived within the context of responsible participation in our world, with all of its ambiguities and its difficult problems. These problems are legion, and many of them are inescapable. Their solutions are rarely easy.

Easy or not, addressing in God's name the moral-laden social issues of our time is an essential aspect of Christian life. A glance at four such issues follows. These are not new developments likely to be judged morally neutral later on. They are inherently troublesome for a Christian.

1. Family Life. The Christian striving for practical sanctity must come to grips with the persistent problems involved in family life. The family is increasingly jeopardized by the growing prevalence of extra-marital sexual relations and other moral perversions of many kinds. These unholy moral deviations are being defended as acceptable parts of the social norm. The Christian must recognize that the right relation between a man and a woman lies at the very heart of society and civilization, and it touches very intimately the integrity of holy life.

Not only must the responsible Christian saint recognize these moral challenges in the abstract; Christians are under heavy obligation to address them seriously in their own homes and elsewhere. In a reasoned, structured, and non-squeamish manner, we must project to the young the beauty and legitimacy of sexual intimacy within marriage, and the destructive and erosive character of extra-marital sex. It is the measured judgment of this author that the people of the Holiness Movement are still seeking a constructive and creative sexual ethic.

2. Sexual Deviations. The so-called "sexual revolution" beginning in the 1960s promises a continuing confrontation between socially accepted practice and the sensitive Christian conscience. Medical research—and we owe to this much good—progresses apace; potential parents now face the free choice of whether or not to permit a pregnancy to continue to full term. Do-it-yourself measures for the "harmless" termination of a pregnancy are not far away, and our children must live in a world becoming highly permissive at this point. The sensitive Christian must grapple with this problem.

In terms of public policy that obligates all people, Christian and not, I profess to have no single and final answer. Rather, I am inclined to believe that no creative solution can be found until at least two factors are given full recognition. First, the prevention of conception is qualitatively different from the termination of a pregnancy, however early the termination occurs. Second, society has as heavy a stake in setting safeguards around the life of the unborn as it has in protecting the lives of its visible citizens. The not-yet-seen human is still human.

It would seem that, while the artificial regulation of conception (by medically approved means) is increasingly recognized as permissible by realistic and sensitive Christians, the arbitrary termination of a pregnancy already begun (except possibly for a pregnancy occasioned by violent assault, an incestuous relationship, or clearly jeopardizing the health of the prospective mother) is to be reprehended. This issue will call for some hardheaded discussion and Spirit-guided decision in the days ahead. To be faced increasingly in American society is the orientation of so many people to their private "rights." This includes the supposed right to do whatever one wants with one's body, regardless of the consequences to the unborn.

3. Affluence. The man or woman who seeks to live the life of Christian sanctity must recognize the problem posed by affluence in today's American society. We can no longer afford the luxury of such oversimplifications like, "After all, property and money are mere things." In reality, property belongs ultimately to God and in no case should it be held unconditionally by any of us. Haggai reminds us that the silver and gold are God's (Hag. 2:8). The Psalmist remarks that God possesses "the cattle on a thousand hills" (Ps. 50:10).

We Christians who live in an affluent society will never get beyond the need for correctives to a steel-tipped sense of ownership. We need constant reminders that the selfish use of property is under God's judgment—whether the selfish use is by the state or by individuals, whether by sinner or saint. The Christian may well find that a certain amount of ownership contributes to a sense of dignity and a feeling of security; but no person in this life can get beyond the potential peril of judging a man's life in terms of "the abundance of that which he possesses."

4. Racism. The "sensitive saint" (and can there be any other kind?) dare not sweep under the rug the disturbing fact that, for over a century since the American Civil War, many of the "saved" and "sanctified wholly" believers have continued to justify racial discrimination, or more hypocritically, to practice it in the name of "good business." This is morally unacceptable in God's eyes. Solutions must be found to racism whether it is found in individual hearts and in social systems that institutionalize and perpetuate it.

Sufficient Saints

In light of the issues we raise here, one naturally asks if there is a sufficiency for these things. Ponder the promise, "If any of you is lacking in wisdom, ask God who gives to all generously and ungrudgingly, and it will be given you" (James 1:5). There also is St. Paul's private assurance received from our Lord, "My grace is sufficient for you, for power is made perfect in weakness" (2 Cor. 12:9). Our dark world needs divine wisdom and grace, and it needs it desperately!

People committed to Christian holiness have a message. It is, we are persuaded, as changeless as God's character and will. But it has little worth as a mere museum piece. The God of Peace, the universe's Holy Sovereign, has been in the business of building saints for a long time, saints who could live adequately in their times. We are persuaded that God stands available, with full resources in hand, to build in our demanding age a type of strong, clear-thinking, and fearless saint who is fully saved and adequately equipped to weather creatively the growing ferocity of the moral storm of this day.

Once the saints have been faithful and the tempest is over, they will stand majestic and unbent and unscarred against the eternal sky. In the meantime, a saint is one filled with the Spirit's presence and wisdom for living responsibly in times like ours.

Questions to Ponder

1. This author says that the Holiness Movement has had a tendency to offer too-easy answers to very hard social questions (as have many others). Recall, for instance, the prohibiting of alcohol sales in the 1920s. Did that solve the evil of drinking in the United States? What about illegal drugs today? What about holiness people prohibiting for themselves things that are morally neutral, like musical instruments in worship? Why would such a prohibition have occurred in the first place?

2. Are the major social evils identified by Harold Kuhn in 1968 still the ones most troubling for Christians today? Have they worsened or improved? Can you name one in particular that still persists and must be addressed with courage?

3. Are Christians guilty of sometimes being mostly a conservative reaction to social change—change being thought of as needing to be resisted just because it is different, unknown, a temptation to "go with the crowd"? Is the crowd always wrong? Can change be avoided in our time of dramatic technological and other advances that seem to be happening constantly?

4. What should anchor Christians in a deeply sinful world? Note the author's final comments on what can make possible "sufficient saints." Are you "fearless" and "fully saved and adequately equipped" to live out your faith creatively and courageously in times like ours?

Chapter 11

Holiness and Dis-Ability:
The Paradox of Power

DIANE LECLERC

Focus: Has the world's concept of power invaded the Christian under-standing of holiness? Does might make right, or at least allow the right to survive in a sinful world? Are we sinful humans "able" to become "per-fect"? Do the strong need the weak even more than the weak need the strong? Living with "disability" present in her own immediate family, Di-ane Leclerc has gained important new insights into what it means to be "perfected in love." The "kenotic" love of God, a voluntary self-giving so unlike the world, displays God's very nature and the meaning of holiness for Christians. We can learn more about this when we move into the arena of dis-ability.

I am concerned with the intersections of suffering, the holy life, and persons we label as "disabled." All of us are familiar with the New Testament references to Paul's physical struggle, which might have been a painful eye condition. Paul tells us in 2 Corinthians 12 that it was a tormenting "thorn in his flesh." He endured it, even though he asked God to heal him three times and God did not. Paul attempts to make some sense of this difficult condition in which he found himself. He searches for answers, as many of us do when we do not understand the suffering we must endure.

Paul did make his way through his own suffering and found a way to take the meaninglessness out of his own physical anguish. He plumbs the very depths of human experience and gives hope to all who feel forsaken in the pool of pain. But he does not finally answer the "why" question. Rather, he answers the "how" question. How do we endure what we never quite understand?

Paradoxically, Paul's bottom line is that "power is made perfect in weakness." Since God's grace is sufficient, somehow we are made perfect while still in weakness. Therefore, he boasted all the more gladly about his weaknesses so that Christ's power might rest on him. That is why he says that, for Christ's sake, "I delight in weaknesses, in insults, in hardships, in persecutions, in difficulties. For when I am weak, then I am strong" (2 Cor. 12:9-10).

A New View of Power

John Wesley appears to have understood what we sometimes do not. He had a category that was neither moral nor immoral. He did not, like Job's friends and so many of our fundamentalist friends, see all suffering as connected to sin. He resisted the claim that poor bodily health implies bad spiritual health. He would not have said to my own father—hospitalized after a traumatic psychiatric break—what one of our locally licensed ministers told him. He announced to my father that, if he would only confess his hidden sin, they could walk out the front doors of the pysch ward together!

John Wesley talked compassionately about our human weaknesses without agonizing over the whys of their origins. "Infirmities," he called them, those wounded and broken and hurting places in our bodies and minds and emotions that do not fall under the rubric of sin. Wesley acknowledged these—in some sense long before such thinking was introduced through the medical and social sciences.

For far too long, we have written theologies of our *abilities*, but they have been theologies that have not included ruminations on what it means to be *disabled*, ruminations sympathetic with those unable to reflect the way we assume life and spirituality "should be." How often do we, as Wesleyan theologians, use metaphors that unconsciously elicit images of disability to describe spiritual failing? I myself have long defined sin as brokenness, holiness as wholeness, thinking that I am using healthier expressions for our doctrine than previous generations—never connecting such language with the denigration of disabled persons. We are prone to use carelessly theological language that in effect demeans disability. How, then, are we different from our predecessors who associated evil with black skin?

Jesus was very clear. In the Kingdom of God, the last will be first; the poor, the mournful, the meek, and the hungry, will be blessed and filled. The powerful in the world will be the least in the Kingdom of God. Indeed, the Kingdom of God turns everything upside down. Authority is redefined. Mastery is minimized. Power is seen in paradox. In fact, the essence of God is *self-emptying love*. It is not in omnipotence, but in his choice toward disability that Jesus reveals God. The cross-centered love of God in Jesus is the same love to which we are called. It is a love that is perfected only in apparent weakness. The *kenotic* (self-emptying) character of God is not irrelevant to us; Jesus' choice to humble himself, dis-able himself, calls us also to come and die—and to respect the "dis-abled" among us.

This leads me to my own fear that living dependently in relation to others will bring me, and other women, disempowerment rather than realizing that it is in this type of dependency and weakness in community that I will find true strength. The disabled people among us, while wishing for "independent living," are often forced to accept dependent relationships for their own survival. May God have mercy on me for ever implying that such dependency equates to sin.

My own son has a form of Autism known as Aspberger's Syndrome. I have watched him struggle. There is a kind of "why" that cries out to

God when the potential of a human life is lost—like that of a life cut short by illness or sickness unto death—the tragedy of human beings who have their health or even their lives stolen from them. This kind of "why" is an agonizing cry. But perhaps just as deep is the cry in the midst of a situation where there never was any "perfect" human potential. The dis-abled simply are not able to reach successfully for something like "spiritual perfection."

I must confess that for most of my professional theological life I have defined "holiness" too narrowly. Let me explain. Central to my theology of holiness have been two theological concepts. First, I have proclaimed that holiness must be defined as fulfilling the command to love God with our whole being, and our neighbor as ourselves, and not just as some sinless perfection. Secondly, I have defined the ability to love as the image of God in us. Thus, the renewal of the image of God is a renewal of our ability to love God and neighbor. That is how I defined the sanctifying and perfecting work of God in our lives.

One fine scholar I know has defined the image of God in us humans as our being "capable of God." I would concur. I believe that this was John Wesley's way of defining the holy life—being capable of loving God and neighbor. But there is a problem. This definition strongly implies an *ability* to choose this higher moral ground. My thoughts and definitions have moved away from an *ability* orientation because of my life experiences with suffering. My son is not "capable of God" in any traditional sense. Does that condemn him to being outside the possibilities of being "holy"?

I believe that there are persons who are so afflicted that they are incapable of what we would normally identify as their own love for God and neighbor. There are several categories of people who cannot consistently choose the wise or, if you will, the "right" moral action. From the severe to the milder forms of various in-abilities, we can label countless persons as unable to choose consistently loving acts; indeed, they are people with diminished capacity for the kind of holiness that many of us have long espoused. Therefore, the question staring me in the face at this juncture is: Do I want to exclude such persons from those created in the image of God? Once again, God have mercy if I answer "yes."

Holiness in Community

In light of such afflicted people, understanding the image of God in us in terms of *capability* is simply inadequate, if not worse. A fresh insight has become helpful to me. While I have always defined the image of God in relational terms, I have not always understood it in *communal* terms. I am only starting to understand what I even mean by that. We are, *as a community*, holy people. We together are the holy, although the broken body of Christ. When one part suffers, all suffer. When one part rejoices, all rejoice. And when one part loves, all love, whether or not each one is "capable" of that loving.

For those incapable of "normal" love, for those trapped in bodies that have betrayed them, or trapped in minds tortured by disorder, I, no WE love them and love for them. We empty ourselves out for them so that they are seen as real persons, as part of the community of faith, as parts of the Body that are just as valuable as we are. Indeed, part of our own humanity is only actualized when we humanize others, treat others as subjects with dignity and not objects over against which we define ourselves.

When we are truly the church, humanizing the abled and disabled alike, the image of God shines forth—not only in our capacities and our abilities, not even in our potentiality that for many has been lost or limited, but as the image of God shines forth from *the church together*. The glow of love shines from the weakness of us all. Christ's body was broken. The church as Christ's body is broken. Since it is, we are to live interdependently, not only relying on each other's strengths, but also, sacramentally and corporately, strong despite each other's weaknesses.

This is the meaning of solidarity so central to our holiness tradition; this is the true community to which God calls the church. It is a meaning of holiness that we have too often ignored because we are tempted to define ourselves in worldly terms—in terms of the economy of power as judged by the world. But in the Kingdom of God we are to redefine power paradoxically in order to reflect the image of God in the church. Even in our weakness, by God's grace and through God's people, we all are strong, even holy.

So we need to ask ourselves hard questions. Does it take more power for us to exert authority over others or to live in reciprocity? Does it take more power to preach against injustice or stand with the oppressed and cry with one of the victims who is in pain? Does it take more power to seek the obviously miraculous or to live quietly and invisibly for the sake of another? Does it take more power to believe that God can raise the dead or to say, "even though you slay me, yet will I trust you"? And to critique my own work: Does it take more power to live independently as a woman before God or to confess my need and live dependent on the broken body of Christ, both in the Eucharist and in the church? Power must be defined differently in the Kingdom of God.

What, Then, Is Holiness?

Christian holiness, then, is not so much defined by a quality in *me*—not even a quality given by God. In this sense, holiness should not be primarily defined as our *ability*, our power to love God. Rather, holiness, down to its very foundations, is about God's *kenotic* (self-emptying) love for us even in our weakness. Under the conditions of human existence, our pain and our suffering show us all as needy. We are not whole. But does this exclude us from holiness? Not if we redefine power paradoxically as weakness. Not if we redefine holiness as communal dependency. Not if we see ourselves and others through God's eyes.

Being "sanctified" does not make us whole in the sense of absolute perfection. It means that we are perfectly loved. God looks with eyes of kenotic love, and we are to look at each other with eyes of kenotic love. We pour ourselves out, as we can, and we are made holy together—not out of a position of power, but precisely because of our position of weakness lived out in a self-emptying community of faith. We treat our unpresentable parts with special honor, and we all are mutually sanctified in the process.

Holiness, under the rubric of weakness, allows us to see that holiness and infirmity are not antithetical. Power and weakness do not stand against each other. Weakness and disability elicit our dependence on God and on each other. The heart of the Christian message remains paradoxical in so many ways. The heart of our holiness message must change if it does not live and breathe in this paradoxical economy of God's power.

I conclude with these wise words from Paul. Christ said to him in his suffering: "My grace is sufficient for you. My power is made perfect in weakness. When you are weak, then you are strong." May it be so!

Questions to Ponder

1. Diane Leclerc speaks of a new view of power, a "kenotic" kind. It is known by us paradoxically and, she says, is key to being truly holy. Try to put in your own words what kenotic means and why it is so essential for understanding Christian holiness.

2. Once our author had explored the paradox of power in Christian life, what resulting change came in her own understanding of holiness? Does this new "weakness" understanding of holiness significantly change your view of the church and the spiritual potential of particular people around you who are labeled as "disabled"?

3. Are you "capable" of God? Does becoming "holy" make you capable of truly loving God and neighbor? What about someone who is significantly disabled in mind or emotions? Is that person disqualified from ever becoming holy? Can you and other brothers and sisters in the faith "add capacity" to the disabled one—love them and love *for them*?

4. What "infirmity" do you have? How can it become a positive ministry for you, and for the able and disabled people around you? Can a "thorn in the flesh" be a special instrument of God's love? What might you do to make your infirmity a ministry for yourself and others?

Chapter 12

Holiness and Women:
The Empowerment of our Foremothers

SUSIE C. STANLEY

Focus: Many conservative Christians, Protestant and Roman Catholic, use their reading of a few New Testament verses to exclude women from some church leadership roles, particularly from being preaching clergy with the full rights of comparable men. The Wesleyan/Holiness Movement has seen something else altogether in Scripture and early church history. It has tried to restore what it sees as the practice of Jesus, the role of women in the early church, and the intention of the Holy Spirit's gifting for service. Does the experience of holiness empower women for priestly leadership? It has been argued that it does not, or at least often has not, but Susie Stanley goes to the personal writings of actual holiness women to demonstrate otherwise.

The Wesleyan/Holiness Movement has sought to model the early church by affirming a prophetic leadership which based its authority on the Holy Spirit. Holiness leaders have been explicit about their intention to imitate the prophetic leadership style of the New Testament era. They have documented the role of women in primitive Christianity and sought to restore to women the prominent place they once filled.

While the prophetic authority of the Holy Spirit held sway initially in the early church, by the second century priestly leadership in the form of a hierarchy composed of presbyters, deacons, and bishops began to squelch prophetic authority. The developing institutional hierarchy situated all authority in its offices. Authority came to be associated with the priestly position (held only by men) rather than flowing directly from the Holy Spirit to called individuals of either gender.

Autobiographies of Prominent Holiness Women

Wesleyan/Holiness women since John Wesley's time have testified to the fact that, for them, empowerment for leadership did accompany the experience of holiness. Their resulting ministries demonstrated the power of the Holy Spirit in their lives. Empowered by God's Spirit, they effectively challenged the ethic of domesticity which sought to confine them within the walls of their homes. Armed with the gift of divine power, women overcame the "man-fearing spirit" and moved outside their homes, refusing to limit their ministries to their immediate families.

Current Christian discussions of the empowerment of women can be enhanced by the awareness of many foremothers in the Wesleyan/Holiness Movement who relied on the empowerment of the Holy Spirit to minister as evangelists and social reformers. Their lives provide a usable past to inspire their daughters of today as they articulate a theology of empowerment that will enable them to fulfill their own callings from God.

My purpose here is two-fold: to introduce more holiness women's autobiographies and to challenge the common assertion that the doctrine of holiness mitigates against women's quest for equality and autonomy. Some have argued that holiness teachings have encouraged disgust among those who have worked for greater autonomy and self-reliance for women. But the reality of the impact of holiness is very different from that in many cases. There are alternative stories of holiness women that deserve careful consideration. For instance, Sarah Cooke (see below) reports that she often met with Christians of deep experience who received their first religious light, especially on holiness, through the lives and writings of various Christian women. She even judged that no books other than the Bible itself were found to be more valuable than the autobiographies of outstanding holiness women. We are fortunate that considerable material exists for our consideration.

John Wesley instructed his followers to write journals, so it is not surprising that many of them left extensive journals, some of which were published after they died. Spiritual autobiography played an important role in Methodist class meetings and worship since exhorters centered on their religious quests, offering the opportunity to formulate an oral account of their lives. Some of these insightful accounts were written by women. The autobiographies of women who worked with John Wesley provide alternative stories for holiness women. Their stories show their engagement in public ministries and their important involvement in their own spiritual growth.

Women were not defensive about writing their life stories because there were precedents within their religious tradition. They addressed an audience that fostered this activity and recognized the importance of autobiographies. One key importance of autobiographies is the subversive implications of such undertakings. Feminist scholars define women's autobiography as a subversive activity because often it challenges the boundaries established by a society that tends to confine women's activities within pre-set and limited boundaries. I will focus briefly on the recorded spiritual journeys of select holiness women and their experiences as *women preachers*. The subversive nature of their experiences will be seen as I concentrate on their successful efforts to challenge the restrictive sphere that society sought to impose on them.

I refer in particular to six holiness women who boldly recorded their "subversive" spiritual journeys. They are:

➢ Mary Still Adams, *Autobiography of Mary Still Adams or, "In God We Trust"* (1893)
➢ Mary Lee Cagle, *Life and Work of Mary Lee Cagle: An Autobiography* (1928)
➢ Mary Cole, *Trials and Triumphs of Faith* (1914)
➢ Sarah A. Cooke, *The Handmaiden of the Lord, or Wayside Sketches* (1896)
➢ Mary A. Glaser, *Wonderful Leadings* (1893)
➢ Alma White, *The Story of My Life and the Pillar of Fire*, 5 vols. (1935–1943)

The Empowered Journeys of Holiness Women

Each of these six women provides an account of her conversion. Their ages at conversion ranged from ten (Adams) to twenty-three (Cooke), with the other four being in their teens. Cole and Cooke were converted through the efforts of siblings, while others experienced conversion in a church setting, either a regular service, a revival, or a camp meeting. These women actively sought conversion, reflecting their Arminian heritage with its emphasis on the freedom of the individual to respond to God's call to salvation. This represents a shift from the spiritual narratives of Puritan women who played a passive part in their conversions, believing that God predestines the elect.

Following conversion, these women pursued the possibility of sanctification, a second distinct work of grace. Like conversion, the quest for sanctification required the seeker to play an active role. Several of the women related sanctification to their subsequent ability to preach. For White, sanctification enabled her to overcome her natural shyness and the "man-fearing spirit" which constrained her when she considered preaching prior to her sanctification. Cagle's process of consecration included the willingness to preach. She had felt called to preach earlier in life, but with sanctification the call "was stronger than ever before."

The power of God's Spirit was required for preaching at a time when this function was usually reserved for a male church hierarchy. The women were well aware of the fact that their preaching defied the prevailing attitude that a woman's proper place was in the home. Their public activities undermined the usual social construction of gender based on claims that women, either by "nature" or by "God's design," could not preach. Women preachers escaped the culturally-constructed sphere which had been designed to confine all women to their "proper" place—which certainly did not include the pulpit. Their escape was assisted by their involvement in the holiness tradition with its emphasis on the empowerment of the Holy Spirit.

Many leaders in the holiness movement endorsed women's preaching. Therefore, women in this tradition faced fewer barriers to preaching than did women in most mainline denominations. Holiness believers often challenged the ideology of gender prevalent in the society around them. Although many may have accepted the conceptions of gender that supported the view that differences were "God given" or "natural," they rejected the prevailing belief that because of these differences only men could preach.

While Cagle professed that God had called her to ministry when she was a child, she initially expected that she would serve as a missionary. After all, this was the only outlet for women's ministry in her church of the time. In her early twenties, she was reclaimed for Christ and "the call came clear and plain," but it was a call to preach in the United States rather than go to a foreign mission field. She preferred the missions option since it would have been much easier than preaching the gospel at home where people were opposed to women fulfilling this leadership role. Adams also hesitated, initially testing her call to preach. If the call were to be judged valid, she asked God for one person to respond to her sermon. Six people came to the altar for salvation following her message. So, for Adams, the matter was settled. God had spoken and acted on her behalf.

Glaser reported finding prejudice everywhere. Her strategy was to leave the issue with the Lord since one day all things would be made right. Cagle and Cole encountered rumors intended to discredit their ministries. In Cagle's case, the male ministers in one city spread falsehoods seeking to terminate a revival she was leading. Referring to herself in the third person, she claimed that "if one-hundredth part that was told on her had been true, she should have been in the penitentiary instead of preaching the gospel." In situations such as this, she relied on the promise of Isaiah 54:17: "No weapon that is formed against thee shall prosper: and every tongue that shall rise against thee in judgment thou shalt condemn. This is the heritage of the servants of the Lord."

Pentecost as the Precedent

Holiness individuals such as Catherine Booth and B. T. Roberts had previously established the Scriptural basis for women preachers. Women relied on this tradition. Defenses for the preaching of women identified Pentecost as the precedent for women's ministry. The Spirit fell on all assembled, regardless of national origin or gender. For a recent and detailed addressing of the New Testament teaching on women and church leadership, see the article by Sharon Pearson in the *Wesleyan Theological Journal* (31:1, 1996) titled "Women in Ministry: A Biblical Vision."

Occasionally, some of these six holiness women claimed the right to more than the privilege of preaching in church. White contended that women should take an active role in the political arena as well as in the religious realm. She celebrated the passage of suffrage for women in 1920 and supported the Equal Rights Amendment when it was first introduced in Congress. White defined "religious and political equality for the sexes" as part of her church's creed and preached against the chains which kept women "in political and ecclesiastical bondage." Her sermon titles on this topic included "Emancipation of Woman" and "Woman's Place in Church and State."

It often has been claimed that holiness teaching has accentuated character traits that kept women docile and yielding. The sanctified people were supposed to be unassertive, selfless, slow to complain, and hardly claiming their rights against prevailing social standards. While some of this might have been applicable to some sanctified women, docile and unassertive hardly describe the six women sampled here. They stepped forward in the power of the Spirit to fulfill their callings, regardless of the opposition of men and the dominating social and religious standards. They dared to be leaders inspired by Pentecost who were called and empowered by God.

Questions to Ponder

1. Should church leadership be based on the control of "official" church bodies or, as Susie Stanley says was true of the early church, "the prophetic leadership of the Holy Spirit"? Can these two options function jointly without humans assuming authority belonging only to God?

2. Empowerment for effective Christian service should come with an experience of true holiness. Recall the experiences of the six women sampled in this chapter. In what forms did empowerment come, and with what results?

3. Have you ever heard it said that Jesus was *meek*, but not *weak*? He was a man with power that was kept under proper control. If one trait of being holy is being humble, does holiness breed an unhealthy compliance with things as they are—sometimes things that are very wrong?

4. Women seeking ordination sometimes are accused of demanding their rights rather than possessing a divine call to ministry. Why is this argument used against women and rarely against men? Do you have a divine calling on your life that you have resisted because of a fear of opposition or failure?

5. Are you open to a woman serving your church in any way that her gifts appear to qualify her—despite any traditional restrictions on that service? Does your church restrict women from any roles merely because they are women? Are you open to a fresh understanding of what the Bible actually teaches on this subject?

Chapter 13

Holiness and Higher Education:
The Importance of Place

MERLE D. STREGE

Focus: Merle Strege discusses higher education in a way that emphasizes the importance of "place" in the intellectual life of colleges and universities. In particular, he focuses on Wesleyan-Holiness institutions of higher education. Academically, colleges and universities are situated in the "place" of a higher educational system that is unconcerned about their particular historical beliefs and values. This may help colleges and universities provide a comparable curriculum throughout the country, but it diminishes the particularities of individual institutions. Strege encourages Christian colleges and universities, especially Wesleyan-Holiness institutions, to allow their beliefs and values to inform and enhance their educational efforts. After all, holiness does not distract from learning; it provides a richness of "place"—a location to be reclaimed, and stories out of which institutions can and should be living.

We have before us now a large and growing body of literature that examines the phenomenon of the church-related or Christian colleges and universities. Recent works by leading evangelical scholars Mark Noll and George Marsden have focused attention respectively on the life of the mind and the secularization of the American university. These two volumes, especially Marsden, have helped us considerably to understand the forces at work on American institutions of higher education, including church-related or Christian universities. In a curious way, both Noll and Marsden themselves bear the marks of such influence. After all, one cannot expect to be taken seriously as an academic unless one's work follows academic conventions and standards.

I wish to pursue a line of thought here that considers an idea related to the following somewhat commonplace observation. Beginning with Stephen Toulmin's observations about the Enlightenment, I want to suggest the importance of "place" in the intellectual life of the universities sponsored by the Wesleyan-Holiness churches.

In his stimulating and provocative analysis of modernity and its agenda, philosopher-physicist Toulmin rejects the Enlightenment's commitments to universal, timeless, general, and written descriptions, predisposed—for example, in *La Grand Encylopedie's* description of René Descartes' philosophical work—as the product of a disembodied mind. Toulmin challenges this predisposition with his own account of a Cartesian philosophical program profoundly shaped by the tumultuous events of early seventeenth-century France. In his view, one cannot conceive of Descartes' revolutionary philosophy, or the work of any other person, apart from the socio-political location it inhabited.

I will draw upon the observations of Toulmin's analysis of Descartes and the Enlightenment to the theme of place and the university in three ways. (1) I will apply Toulmin's description of Descartes to my own institution, Anderson University, and comparable Wesleyan-Holiness institutions to say, first, that descriptions of the university abstracted from its social and intellectual location make no more sense than the French encyclopedia's article on Descartes. (2) The second connection will be a prescriptive argument correlative to the first point: universities should practice a politics, a way of being together, that embodies the intellectual traditions of their constituent communities. (3) Third, I want to suggest a description of the possible politics of Anderson University, a university sponsored by the Church of God (Anderson, Indiana). It is the Wesleyan-Holiness movement institution with which I am most familiar. This description will entail the notion that at least some part of our intellectual life will draw upon salient theological notions of the Church of God, resulting in their contribution to the shape of the university's politics.

On the Social and Political Locations of Colleges and Universities

Perhaps it is only in the United States that the standardization of university education is believed to be desirable. Medieval universities differed markedly in subject matter and governance. Bologna, Paris, and Oxford resembled each other hardly at all, each of them giving institutional expression to quite different intellectual and political traditions. In a similar fashion, intellectual and political commitments distinguished early twentieth-century European universities from one another. For example, in the 1920s, the reigning theology in Göttingen was anathema at Berlin. In the United States, however, and especially among schools that are dominated by undergraduate studies, claims of institutional distinction are based not in intellectual differences, but in assertions of superiority.

I suspect that one answer to this question might be located in the dominance of the academic and professional guilds in American higher education. Accreditation, whether by regional or professional associations, tends to blur institutional distinctiveness as it standardizes the programs offered by its related institutions. If this is the case, we find ourselves in the rather odd position of saying that, as concerns curriculum—the heart of our universities—an Anderson education will not differ substantially from what a student might get at nearby Ball State University or Goshen College.

The present situation of American higher education, then, seems a denial of the historical, social, and political particularities of individual colleges and universities. Such a denial is as unfaithful to historical circumstance as it is undesirable. That an ahistorical approach dominates American higher education is, however, not surprising. Ameri-

can culture has deep roots in the Enlightenment, the premium it places on instrumental reason, and its denial of importance to that which
"enlightened" thinkers judge to be local, time bound, particular, or
oral.

In his insightful essay "The Loss of the University," Wendell Berry
argues that universities have lost sight of a common goal to which
their specific departments might be oriented. Even worse, he contends,
is that universities have lost the common language that enabled their
members to converse about the ends for which their institutions exist.

The accuracy of Berry's analyses is born out when we ask: What
then holds universities together in the absence of a common language? The most common American answer to this question is "the
university administration." The common language of the American
university then becomes "administrationese": GPA, FTE, FAF, major,
minor, GRE, outcomes assessment, and the like. Such a move gives up
the language of ends for the language of instrumental reason.

I submit that it makes no historical sense to deny the very real differences that distinguish American colleges and universities from one
another. These differences should be understood as extending beyond
the quantifiable, unless we believe that the determinative difference
between Anderson and Goshen, for example, is that the library at one
of them has more holdings than the other. Such homogenization de-
values the specific historical and social locations of educational institutions that actually are quite diverse and deserve to be so recognized.

Universities as Embodied Intellectual Traditions

I am not suggesting that we flout the recommendations and standards
imposed by our learned societies, and professional and regional ac-
crediting associations. But is it not reasonable to ask that the moral,
religious, and intellectual traditions of any particular college or university modify or contextualize these external forces, thereby adapting
them to particular institutional landscapes?

In the case of church-related colleges and universities, this means
that their work will need to be informed in some way by the theological traditions of the sponsoring church groups. I am not issuing a call
for each and every course to have a religious or a spiritual component.

Neither is it desirable that religion be the only acceptable discourse on the campus.

Theological Traditions of the Church of God (Anderson)

Notions such as the categories of holiness, experience, community, and vocation have been important elements in the theological tradition of the Church of God. They also have affinities with other colleges and universities of the Wesleyan-Holiness tradition. I suggest that these four categories also might inform intellectual life and institutional politics at Anderson University.

(1) "Holiness" surely is an idea deserving of informing ethics and moral philosophy, but perhaps also courses in public policy or political science. To be sure, the Church of God (Anderson) along with many other Wesleyan-Holiness groups has, in the main, conceived the idea of holiness in moralistic and individualist terms. But in Walter Brueggemann's recently published volume, *Old Testament Theology*, we find an example of how such traditional and conservative notions of holiness might be enlarged to undergird important political, economic, and ethical themes. Brueggemann demonstrates the relationships between Israel's conception of God, its understanding of its own social location "among the nations," and God's evolving commitment to justice and righteousness as expressions of God's holiness. To follow Brueggemann's lead will mean that the idea of holiness, whether of God or God's people, will inform discussions in areas such as ethics, economics, theories of management, and public policy.

(2) Anderson University professors such as Willard Reed (philosophy) have interpreted the Church of God movement's theological idea of experience in a manner which bears directly on the university's intellectual life. Reed observes that the Church of God has long maintained an epistemology that places experience ahead of rationalistic conceptions about knowledge. Furthermore, he contends that, insofar as faith is concerned, members of the Anderson University faculty need not be threatened by rationalistically framed propositions since they cannot threaten religious experience. Reed has interpreted a sali-

ent theological idea of the Church of God in a manner which clearly underwrites the freedom essential to academic inquiry and debate.

(3) The surest illustration of my point is that no Anderson faculty appointment is conditional on a signature of confession or creed. That faculty members are not required to sign a belief statement is not due to the Enlightenment-based notion that one's religious commitments are private. Rather, it is precisely because Anderson University is shaped by the ethos of the Church of God, a part of which is that one's religious experience cannot be reduced to a set of propositions. Therefore, faculty members will not be required to sign a creed. The same could not be said at all member institutions of the Coalition for Christian Colleges and Universities.

(4) One last theme important to the theological life of the Church of God has been the tradition of vocation. It is, of course, the case that the idea of calling has been important throughout Christianity. I am not claiming that the concept is unique to the Church of God. But the idea has nevertheless received considerable stress and broad interpretation among us. The Church of God has thought of people's vocations largely in terms of the ministry; men and women receive a "call to full-time Christian service," as we often have said. But vocation could also be extended beyond the sacred to the secular, and in its earlier years Anderson University played an important role in broadening the meaning of vocation to include gainful employment in service to a particular place.

Conclusion

We appear to face a choice between two modes of being: either we will ground ourselves in the traditions and politics of our larger church communities, or we will speak the discourses of non-church systems that claim to provide the solution to our problems. Out of that identity, we must be able to answer the question, "What are we to do?"

Today institutions of Christian higher education especially should be answering the same vital question. For those colleges and universities whose historic identities lie in the Wesleyan-Holiness tradition, there is richness to be recovered, an important location to be reclaimed, and stories out of which institutions can and should be living.

Questions to Ponder

1. How would you describe your "place" in the world? In particular, how would you describe your Christian "place"?

2. Do you agree that a Christian college or university's "place" should influence it education? How? To what extent?

3. What spiritual strengths did you gain from the "place" (for example, family, church, education) in which you grew up? What spiritual strengths do you have in your current "place"?

4. How may we improve our "place" in the world? In particular, how may we promote holiness more in the "place" in which we live? in our church? in our community?

5. How may we improve the "place" of education, even when it occurs in a secular context? How should education in a Christian context differ from education in a secular context?

Chapter 14

Holiness and Public Perception: Sanctification in Contemporary Films

THOMAS E. PHILLIPS

Focus: As a Wesleyan reared in a conservative holiness tradition, Thomas Phillips and many others spelled "cinema" with an "s" (*SIN*ema). As so many once taught, real Christians do not smoke, drink, dance, play cards, or go to movies. Holiness must be taken seriously. It was, in part, a matter of public perception—one did not want to be known as associating with evil. Today, many holiness people, still intending to exercise discrimination in their lifestyles, do go to theaters or watch films on TV or on one of their other electronic devices. The perennial issue is this. How does one live *in* the world but not be *of it*? How does one avoid destroying a witness for Christ by engaging in actions that would be perceived as hypocritical by the public? Should Christians today frequent movie theaters? If they do, what should they watch and how is their faith being portrayed to the public on the big screen? Some films that are very influential on public opinion focus on holiness themes—and often not favorably. Phillips samples the field and chooses to highlight three films that present—subtly— differing views of salvation and the holy life.

The medium of film has long been recognized as an excellent means of engaging in cultural critique. The church, as a leading institution of Western culture, has never been immune to such critique. Cinematic critique of the church reached previously unparalleled heights in 1960 when Stanley Kramer's legal drama, *Inherit the Wind*, and Richard Brooks' satire, *Elmer Gantry*, both highlighted the church's bigotry, hypocrisy, and anti-intellectualism. Both films garnered well-deserved Oscars for their achievements. Such critiques are not necessarily detrimental (or even hostile) to the church. In fact, they often have the potential of serving as a prophetic voice to a complacent church.

A Wesleyan/Holiness approach to Christian faith calls for the opening of one's life to the possibility of human moral transformation. Genuine repentance, a human act of response to divine initiatives of grace, frees the believer from the domination of sin and opens the believer to love God and neighbor—freely, sincerely, and consistently. But this potential has its public vulnerabilities. The public media is quick to critique religious "perfectionists" who are living below their ideals and the great possibilities they claim for God's life-changing grace.

After several years of crass cinematic critiques of the church (e.g., *Dogma*, *Stigmata*), we more recently (1999–2004) have experienced a wealth of more sophisticated critiques. Several films have appeared that rival the 1960 masterpieces. Here we examine three of these films that are representative of contemporary cinematic critiques of the church. All three are well-crafted and stingingly powerful. While I enjoy a healthy dose of theologically responsible self-criticism, I find the first two films wanting—not because they fail to critique the church effectively and fairly, but because they do so from a distinctly non-Wesleyan point of view. Let me explain how the criticisms of the church in the very popular *Saved!* and *Mystic River* assume Lutheran and Reformed doctrines of sanctification respectively. In contrast to these commercially successful films, the little known film *Big Kahuna* offers a rare Wesleyan critique of the church.

Saved!: A Lutheran Comedy

Just after Mel Gibson's sadistic *Passion of the Christ* (2004) wowed guilt-ridden Evangelical audiences *en masse*, Brian Dannelly's *Saved!* (2004) offered a satirical look at the dysfunctional American Eagle Christian High School. The plot revolves around the experiences of Mary (Jena Malone) and her failed attempt to "cure" her gay boyfriend Dean (Chad Faust). With all the mixed motives of early adolescence, Mary sneaks into her beau's bedroom and engages him in the delights of her feminine wiles. To her horror, not only does this mid-afternoon tryst not cure Dean of his homosexual impulses, but it leaves Mary with morning sickness. To make matters worse, Dean's parents discover some of his homoerotic pornography and send him to "Mercy House" where Christian counselors have the supposed ability to cure people with Dean's "spiritually toxic affliction."

As Mary's ill-fated scheme unravels and she progresses through the increasingly obvious signs of pregnancy, knowledge of her shame becomes the plot device which separates the sheep from the goats. What unfolds is a sometimes hilarious critique of the church's failures and foibles. Some of the one-liners are delightful—in a hilarious and impious sort of way. Some of the scenes reflect the kind of teen camp spirituality all too often found at Christian high schools and colleges.

I believe that this film's understanding of salvation and sanctification is non-Wesleyan; it is Lutheran. The film does not make me uncomfortable as a Christian; it makes me uncomfortable as a Wesleyan. For both the characters Cassandra and Roland, all of their self-designations are non-Christian, yet all of their actions are compassionate—that is, supposedly Christian. These two characters embody the classic Lutheran views of a believer being "sinner" and "saint" simultaneously. Cassandra and Roland, the self-described sinners, are presented simultaneously as the real saints.

In the world of *Saved!*, salvation begins and ends with the simple recognition that "I am not OK." The saint who emerges from this confession also remains—in typical Lutheran fashion—a sinner. This movie criticizes the church's hypocrisy, but replaces that hypocrisy with no genuine righteousness. Thus, Mary's final words to Pastor Skip summarize the film's Lutheran perspective. Mary insists: "It's just all too

much to live up to. No one fits in 100% of the time . . . not even you."
One admits one's sin and failure and then just lives in that sin and
failure—not a very Wesleyan perspective.

As a Wesleyan, I recognize that the Christian life must always be
characterized by genuine repentance, but I also believe that God's
grace is able to transform lives and produce hearts that can—by the
grace of God—"live up to" the high claims of the gospel. I desire a
greater optimism of grace and a more positive doctrine of sanctification than I find in *Saved!*.

Mystic River: A Calvinist Drama

Clint Eastwood's Oscar winning *Mystic River* (2003) offers another
powerful critique of the church. The central characters struggle to live
a good life in spite of the lasting wounds inflicted upon them by the
church during their youth. The central character, Jimmy, is portrayed
as a guy who wants to share in the church's communion and to do
what is right. In spite of his desire to live well, Jimmy eventually mur-
ders his high school buddy, Dave, when Jimmy becomes convinced
that Dave is guilty of the brutal murder of Jimmy's 19-year-old daughter.

The key scene for understanding the doctrine of sanctification in
this movie appears after Jimmy has learned of Dave's innocence. Jimmy's wife walks into his bedroom where his back is literally covered by
a large tattoo of the cross. In hushed and loving tones, she then begins
assuring Jimmy of his basic goodness—in spite of his tearful admis-
sion: "I killed Dave." I remain uncomfortable with the righteousness
imputed to Jimmy in the wake of Dave's murder. Jimmy can—and
did!—do wrong. He is not a "king;" he is a killer.

As a Wesleyan, I am dissatisfied with any righteousness which is
merely imputed, in spite of all evidence to the contrary. Here is a typically Reformed view. I want genuine righteousness, created and sustained by the transforming grace of God through Jesus Christ.

The Big Kahuna: A Wesleyan Chatroom

I once was asked to list for a university publication my five favorite
films. At the top of the list stood John Swanbeck's barely noticed *The*

Big Kahuna (1999). This film stands out from the typical Hollywood fare for several reasons. Let me list a few.

First, this film has no violence, nudity, sex, or slow-motion explosions. Second, it focuses on only three characters. Phil Cooper (Danny Devito), Bob Walker (Peter Facinelli), and Larry Mann (Kevin Spacey). Their largely cerebral conversations occur in a cheesy hotel room. The film is almost devoid of action. In these and other ways, this film is decidedly not typical Hollywood. It offers what I consider a Wesleyan critique of the church and a Wesleyan doctrine of sanctification—and not because of the setting or lack of action!

Throughout the film Bob is the self-identified but entirely unreflective Christian. He promotes his Baptist faith and seeks to live up to its ideals through zealous evangelism. Bob claims that he has never smoked a cigarette or touched hard liquor, although he "drinks a beer every now and then." Consistent with his sincere faith, Bob sits caressing a Bible while talking to Larry about Phil's divorce. Bob has earlier reminded Phil that his wife was given to him for a "helpmate." In keeping with Bob's piety, when Larry teases Bob about going into a strip club, Bob insists that he has "never even been near a place like that." Larry eventually teases Bob, telling him that he should become a saint because he "wouldn't think about lusting after a woman."

It is Bob's character that introduces the movie's most important theological theme. In conversation with Phil, Bob muses: "I wonder how a person attains character. You know, whether it's something that you're born with and it kind of reveals itself over time or whether you have to go through certain things." After introducing this weighty theme, however, the film shifts focus toward its primary plot device—this trio's need to meet the "Big Kahuna," the president of a major company whose business is essential to their own financial well-being. Their plan is simple. They will host a cocktail party and Bob will tend bar while Larry and Phil search the crowd for the Big Kahuna. After they identify their target, the two will get him to commit to buying their industrial lubricants and all will be well.

In the key scene, Phil and Bob return to the central question of character as Phil shows Bob that Bob has not yet attained character. Phil explains that Bob has no character because he has "no regrets."

Bob, of course, objects and asks if he could only attain by going out and doing something that he would regret. Phil replies that Bob has already done plenty to regret, he just doesn't recognize those things. Phil explains that, when people have regrets, those regrets change them. They form character. In absence of such character, Bob's witness to Christ amounts to little more than a "sales pitch," like a salesman's attempt to promote industrial lubricants. In my judgment, this is Wesleyan repentance in believers and genuine moral transformation.

Finally, here is a Wesleyan critique of the church, a critique that chastises the church for replacing genuine love with manipulation, for failing to actually participate in the broken heart of God, and for reducing the gospel of Christ to a mere "pitch." Finally, in this extraordinary film, we find a Wesleyan understanding of sanctification, an understanding in which genuine repentance brings genuine moral transformation. Rather than having confession as an end unto itself (as in the Lutheran *Saved!*) or confession as a prelude to the fiction of imputed righteousness (as in the Reformed *Mystic River*), *The Big Kahuna* gives us a theology in which confession is followed by genuine moral transformation and a life of love.

Questions to Ponder

1. At issue here are the important subjects of Christian witness and evangelism. If Christians sometimes are abused by the public media, should they boycott the media or turn around and use it for communicating the good news of Jesus Christ?

2. The public is quick to critique religious "perfectionists" who live below their high standards. Since Christianity is prominent in North American society, it is no surprise that Hollywood often takes notice and dramatizes its judgments. Should holiness people reach for less than the ideal of "perfect love" despite the price likely to be paid in public perception?

3. What is said to be theologically inadequate about *Saved!*, the Lutheran comedy? What about the Reformed (Calvinist) drama *Mystic River*? Have you seen a movie lately that consciously furthers or fairly critiques Christian life today? What is its title?

4. What theology is said to be conveyed through the movie *The Big Kahuna*? What is especially "Wesleyan" about this theology? Would a non-religious viewing public catch this implied theological message? How could Christians convey important theological messages without engaging in mere manipulative "pitches"?

5. Should holiness people care about what the public thinks of their counter-cultural beliefs, values, and practices? If they should, what can they do to project the proper image? In particular, what could you do in relation to the public immediately around you? Are you willing to take the risk?

PART 4

CHURCH LIFE AND HOLINESS

Chapter 15

Holiness and Worship:
Focusing on the Holy God

HENRY H. KNIGHT III

Focus: Competing styles of worship have troubled the contemporary Christian community. Should we design worship services in a "classical" way that honors the great tradition of the church? Or, instead, should we design them in a "contemporary" way that tries to remove all barriers to those outside the church by championing popular culture and people's felt needs? Or is there a third option, a better one, one that simultaneously sanctifies the past and the present? According to Henry Knight, the issue should not be traditional or contemporary, but intentional focus on the holy God in order for worshippers to encounter and share in that divine holiness.

Today's congregations are struggling with a real tension that runs through their practice of worship. There appear to be two options of worship "styles." They tend to apply two entirely different sets of criteria for evaluating the adequacy of worship. The first is governed by the aesthetic sensibilities of a pastor and choir director, one or both trained in classical music, who see worship as the occasion for bringing their best and the best of the Christian tradition before God. The second, driven by the desire to share the gospel with those outside the church, seeks to remove all cultural barriers to their comfortable participation, thus deciding against the classical, traditional, and highest quality of presentation. The style of the current culture, typically that of younger people, is now being emphasized widely.

A God-Centered Option

I take very seriously both the concern to be rooted in our faith tradition, to maintain our identity as Christians, and the concern for contextualization, to be relevant to our current culture. The problem is that, while the issues are real, the proposed solutions are often one-sided. Their fundamental problem is that they frame the question wrongly as a presumed choice between "traditional" and "contemporary" worship, or between worship which reflects "high" culture and worship that features "popular" culture.

Instead of letting aesthetic or utilitarian concerns provide the governing criteria for evaluating worship, I propose understanding the central purpose of worship as *the glorification of God and the sanctification of humanity*. Choosing this purpose has distinct advantages for evaluating Christian worship, especially for those in the Wesleyan tradition. For example, it suggests an obvious two-fold test: (1) does our worship glorify God and (2) does it encourage and enable the sanctification of the participants?

I am suggesting that, in proper Christian worship, we should be encouraged and enabled to encounter the God as revealed in Jesus Christ, who is present by way of the Holy Spirit and made known to us through faith, which is a gift of the Holy Spirit. Thus, through the worship experience, we do not simply know *more about* God, but we come to *know God* ever more deeply. This God is not simply an amorphous feeling, but a God who has a distinctive character revealed in Scripture. Authentic worship, then, not only remembers who God is but encounters the living reality of that God through the Spirit. At the same time, it avoids the extremes of a formalism, which simply goes through the motions, and an enthusiasm that substitutes enjoying feelings for knowing God.

It is for this reason that worship that glorifies God *also sanctifies the participants.* Worship that at its heart is utilitarian, or aesthetic, or entertainment cannot sanctify because it does not really glorify—it doesn't remember the God of Israel and of Jesus Christ as the ground and motive for its thanksgiving and praise. Worship that really remembers God in Christ cannot but give God thanks and praise, and in the process it evokes in its participants ever-growing love, hope, humility, joy, peace, and gratitude in response to the love that God has so richly shown in creation, and especially in redemption through Jesus Christ.

My central point is that focusing on the holy God in worship sanctifies those who worship. For this point to be accepted, it is important to understand how I see the glorification of God being related to the sanctification of humanity. Worship that centers in the glorification of God sanctifies the worshippers through forming and shaping in them distinctively *Christian affections.* By contrast, when worship has as its overriding purpose evangelism, therapy, social activism, or any other human-centered goal, it neither glorifies God nor sanctifies persons. It becomes human-centered rather than God-centered. Authentic, sanctifying Christian worship is necessarily centered on God.

Bringing Yesterday Alive Today

Remembering is crucial to Christian worship. We speak of remembering in a special way. It is remembering as *anamnesis,* not a mere recalling to mind of a past event or person that is no longer present. Rather, *anamnesis* is remembrance in which the event or person *becomes present to us.* It is something like experiencing that event or person anew, as a present reality. All remembrance of what God has done is linked in Wesleyan theology with what God will do. In Wesleyan worship there is special focus on the divine promises of pardon and holiness. These are consistently related to God--what God has done in Christ, what God is doing through the Spirit, and what God will do in the end. Recalling the God of yesterday brings alive for us the God of today and tomorrow, the God who is in the saving and sanctifying business.

With the central focus on God as known in Jesus Christ, the natural human responses are praise and thanksgiving. Praising God and giving thanks to God keep all of worship centered on God's character and activity rather than on our own human agendas. Apart from this centering, confession can easily become cheap grace and intercession a personal wish list. When authentic praise and thanksgiving govern our worship, the remembrance of God is central. Confession is a response to being accountable to this God, and intercession is bringing the world before the God who created, loves, and wishes to redeem.

I emphasize authentic praise and thanksgiving because not everything that goes by these names is integrally related to appropriate, God-centered remembrance. Sometimes what is called praise is only lively singing cast adrift from the biblical story of God in Israel and Christ. It may be celebratory, but the reason for celebration remains unclear. Even Scripture choruses can have this effect unless those singing them have some sense of the biblical accounts from which they were extracted. "Exciting" worship does not always direct us to God. This fact is not, however, a blanket condemnation of exuberant worship in favor of a more solemn worship style. Rather, it suggests as one criterion for worship, whatever the style, the question of remembrance. Does it tell us who God is? Does it set before us the God revealed in Scripture?

This brings us back to the original thesis, that worship is both for the glorification of God and the sanctification of persons, but it can only aid the latter if its focus is on the former. We are now in a position to see the relation between the glorification of God in worship and the important result of the sanctification of those who worship. John Wesley understood the Christian life as a pattern of affections or "holy tempers" rooted and grounded in the hearts of believers. I have come to describe these affections as having three characteristics.

First, they are dispositions—abiding inclinations in the heart which characterize us as persons. Thus, to be Christian is to have and be growing in certain affections such as love of God, love of neighbor, faith, hope, humility, gratitude, joy, and the like. Affections as dispositions are to be distinguished from what we today often term feelings. While one may or may not feel loving or thankful at a particular time, to be a Christian is to be a loving and thankful person. The affections are deeper in our character than feelings which come and go; they abide in the heart and remain over time.

Second, affections provide a certain perspective on the world. In a way, they mediate our experience. When we experience a hungry child, it matters greatly whether one's life is characterized by selfishness or compassion. Affections provide us with a way of evaluating our experience as well as the motive to act on that understanding. If asked why we are involved in combating world hunger, the reason we are likely to give is that we have compassion for those who suffer.

Third, affections are intrinsically relational—they take objects. One does not simply love, one loves someone or something. Christians love God and neighbor; they do not love money—or at least struggle with the latter while growing in the former. In the case of an object who is a subject, the relationship can be two-way: we are the objects of God's love; we love God in return.

The relationality of the affections is central to our consideration of worship and sanctification. We cannot have Christian affections apart from an ongoing relationship with God. To forget, ignore, or reject God is to replace God with some other object of our love. When the object of the love changes, the affection of love and the resulting life change as well. The object forms and shapes the affections. Thus, to love the God revealed in Jesus Christ has a profound formative effect on who we are—it is what makes us Christians in the Wesleyan sense of holiness of heart and life. In contrast, to love money would make us very different people, leading lives reflecting values and priorities at variance from those of the gospel.

Remembering Experientially

If the affections are the content of sanctification, and they are formed and shaped by their object, holiness of heart and life is dependent on our remembering *experientially* the God who is holy. Here is the essential link between worship and sanctification: it is as we praise and thank God that, through remembering again and again who God is and what God has done, we grow in the knowledge and love of God. Our own lives are continually shaped and our affections deepened over time by our encounter with this God. As we bring our whole lives to worship God, we render our lives worshipful. This is the essential interrelation of liturgy and ethics, or, in John Wesley's language, of acts of piety and acts of mercy.

I am suggesting that in worship we encounter the God revealed in Jesus Christ, who is present by way of the Holy Spirit, and made known to us through faith, which is a gift of the Holy Spirit. Thus, we do not simply know more about God, but we come to know God ever more deeply; and this God is not simply an amorphous feeling, but a God who has a distinctive character revealed in Scripture. Authentic worship, then, not only remembers who God is but encounters the living reality of that God through the Spirit. Worship should avoid both the extremes of formalism, which simply goes through the motions, and an enthusiasm that substitutes enjoying feelings for really knowing God.

It is for this reason that worship which glorifies God also sanctifies the participants. Worship that at its heart is utilitarian, or aesthetic, or entertainment cannot sanctify because it doesn't really glorify—it doesn't remember the God of Israel and of Jesus Christ as the ground and motive for its thanksgiving and praise. Worship that remembers this God cannot but give God thanks and praise, and evoke in its participants ever-growing love, hope, humility, joy, peace, and gratitude in response to the love that God has so richly shown in creation and especially in redemption through Jesus Christ.

Questions to Ponder

1. Have you or the congregation where you worship gotten caught in a troubled tension between "traditional" and "contemporary" worship styles? Has the result been helpful or harmful? What might have helped to lessen any negative tension?

2. Do you understand Henry Knight's identification of a third option, a "holy" way out of this too-often painful tension? State this third option in your own words.

3. How does this author think that "worship choruses" should be defined if they are to be elements of true worship and not just stimulating entertainment?

4. Is the proper choice between "exciting" worship and more "solemn" worship? What criterion does the author say is proper for determining what is appropriate biblical worship and what is not?

5. What are "affections"? How are they related to worship and sanctification, to what we truly value and choose to remember most of all?

Chapter 16

Holiness and African-Americans: Holiness/Pentecostal Worship

Cheryl J. Sanders

Focus: John Wesley did not wish to be considered an "enthusiast," someone who allows spiritual "experience" to run wild and excessively dominate a Christian's way of knowing and worshipping. Even so, he placed clear importance on experiencing real life change by God's grace, with that change being allowed to truly express itself in worship. Energetic episodes of rejoicing in worship have appeared especially in the African-American and Pentecostal expressions of the Wesleyan/Holiness tradition. These lively expressions are common because numerous African-American believers have been drawn to the holiness emphasis and naturally have brought to church with them their distinctive culture. In addition, numerous holiness believers of all races and human cultures have valued a range of "pentecostal" worship practices.

Worship in the African-American Holiness and Pentecostal churches involves song, speech, dance, and other ways of knowing God and verifying spiritual revelation. This tradition thrives on the integration of aesthetics (cultural authenticity), ethics (implementation of Christian norms), and epistemology (ways of knowing) in its characteristic verbal and bodily articulations of praise. When a soloist or instrumentalist has pushed the congregation to the brink of ecstasy with an inspired performance, when the preacher has brought the sermon to a dramatic climax, when the gatekeepers of pulpit and pew usher the people through the experience of the shout, it is understood as the "witness of the Spirit," the much sought-after manifestation of the Holy Spirit. The underlying ethical and theological context of Holiness-Pentecostal worship is the corporate testimony of being "saved, sanctified, and filled with the Holy Ghost."

I have analyzed my own observations concerning this worship tradition based on data gathered from 1990–1994 during visits to 75 churches and 28 college campuses in 21 states (and the District of Columbia), representing twenty-five Protestant, Catholic, Pentecostal, and Holiness denominations. Based on this information, I have developed a composite portrait of worship in the Holiness-Pentecostal tradition, with attention to eight basic elements: (1) call to worship; (2) songs and hymns; (3) prayer; (4) offerings; (5) Scripture reading; (6) preaching; (7) altar call; and (8) benediction.

The Basic Elements of Worship

The *call to worship* includes acts that initiate the worship experience. It may be a simple and informal verbal signal to "stop chatting and settle down," or a formal combination of choral introit and litany recited by minister and congregation. The call to worship may be a brief reading from the Bible, the church's hymnal, or from some printed worship aid that encourages people to become focused on worship. In some cases it is preceded by a devotional service, including songs, prayers, and testimonies. Also, it may be immediately followed with a processional of the clergy and choir.

The *singing* of some combination of songs, hymns, choruses, and Negro spirituals is a vital part of all these worship services. It is difficult to denote the role music plays in worship with any degree of precision because music tends to undergird everything else that is done. Music is interspersed throughout the service. The singing of songs and hymns represents a major component of congregational involvement in the worship experience. The sung repertoire of the tradition includes classical anthems, arias, oratorios, hymns, gospel songs, spirituals, shouts, chants, and lined-out common-meter sacred folk songs. The call and response between preacher and organist is actually a three-way conversation involving preacher, congregation, and musician. In the hands of an accomplished musician, the organ sings, speaks, and dances.

Prayer is an individual or collective appeal to God, which includes praise, thanksgiving, confessions, and various petitions. As is the case with music, it is difficult to fix one point in the outline of worship where prayer occurs. It typically is done repeatedly throughout the service. Prayers are sometimes chanted in the Pentecostal churches in a manner not unlike the chanted sermon. They are seldom read or recited from a printed source, with the exception of the Lord's Prayer, which the worshippers may recite or chant from memory.

Offerings are taken by having the worshippers march to the front of the sanctuary to deposit their monetary gifts in baskets, plates, or on a table. Also, the ushers may pass the offering receptacles up and down the rows of seated congregants in a precise, orderly fashion. Most of the African-American Holiness and Pentecostal churches emphasize tithing, and sometimes special prominence is given to the tithers by having them come forward individually to place their tithes in a special receptacle. The offerings can consume a considerable amount of time if the minister makes an appeal for a specific cause or if people are asked to bring their offerings according to the specific dollar amount. Usually some form of prayer and/or doxology is offered in connection with the offering, either before or after the monies are actually received.

Scripture reading is another indispensable element in African-American Holiness and Pentecostal worship. One or more texts may be read near the beginning of the service or shortly before the sermon is preached. The Scriptures can be individually read from the pulpit or read responsively by minister and congregation. The Bible is accorded the highest respect in these churches, and in some cases there are special ritual procedures for transporting and handling the particular Bible from which the sermon is preached.

Preaching is a climactic event in this worship tradition because it is believed that the preacher actually speaks for God. Often the sermons are *performed* in the sense that the basic message and content are amplified through chants, moans, dancing, and other ecstatic behaviors. Preaching is more than the simple verbal communication of the gospel of Jesus Christ based on some Scriptural text; it involves emotion, physical movement, various modulations of the preacher's voice, and is designed to bring the worshipping community into some form of climactic expression—shouting, tears, praise, repentance, and/or tongue-speaking. In some of the churches, specific provision is made for the preacher (typically male) to have an attendant (typically female) whose responsibility is to assist him with his liturgical cape, to administer juice or water as needed, to wipe the sweat from his brow, etc., adding to the dramatic impact of the preaching performance. The sermon is always intended to elicit congregational response.

Altar call is a formal ritual of response to the preached word. It usually functions as an invitation to discipleship. Many African-American Holiness and Pentecostal churches adhere to the practice of issuing dual altar calls—the first an appeal for sinners to repent and receive salvation and the second an invitation for believers to receive sanctification or the baptism of the Holy Spirit. Altar calls may also include the ritual laying of hands upon the sick or distressed, and anointing with oil for the purpose of achieving healing or deliverance. In some churches the major objective of the altar call is to invite the worshippers to have hands laid on them so they can be "slain in the Spirit." The dissociative experience of temporary loss of consciousness represents a form of ritual empowerment. There are preachers who invest as much time and energy in directing the altar call as in preaching the sermon.

Benediction is a prayer or formula of blessing signaling that the worship experience has ended. It may include a final exhortation or commission of the worshippers to implement some particular truth or principle that has been preached. The minister who offers the benediction may raise one or both hands, and in some cases the worshippers also raise their hands while receiving the benediction.

Fixed and Fluid Worship

There are some additional aspects of African-American Holiness and Pentecostal worship that distinguish these churches from the white North American Protestant mainstream. The list would include: (1) the holy dance; (2) the "Yes" chant; and (3) the use of white uniformed liturgical attendants. Worship has fixed and fluid forms, rehearsed and unrehearsed, scripted and improvised, prepared and spontaneous. To make matters more complex, it is clear that some forms and events in worship reflect both fixed and fluid elements at the same time.

For example, the quintessential ecstatic expression in Pentecostal worship is the shout or holy dance which usually occurs as a spontaneous eruption into coordinated, choreographed movement. There are characteristic steps, motions, rhythms, and syncopations associated with shouting. It is not a wild and random expression of kinetic energy. Rather, there is a culturally and aesthetically determined static structure which sustains the expression of ecstasy in a definite, recognizable form.

Among black Protestant churches in general, there are two basic orientations toward worship that set the tone for worship in particular congregations: quietistic and lively. The quietistic congregations give priority to static structures, while the lively congregations value ecstatic expressions in worship. Quietistic worship traditions may exclude or control ecstatic worship forms in several ways, for instance by insisting that everything in worship be scripted, read, and timed; by restricting rhythm and repetition, especially in singing; or by direct intervention or verbal rebuke by authorized figures such as ushers or preachers. Lively worship traditions may devalue static worship forms by making statements such as, "We are not here for form or fashion, we are here to praise the Lord," or by vigorously exhorting persons to speak aloud, stand, raise hands, shout, etc., and subjecting them to verbal ridicule if they refuse, as in "You think you're too cute and too sophisticated to shout." The quietistic worship leader imposes silence and stillness upon the congregation; the leader of lively worship invokes noise and motion.

Static and ecstatic worship have their distinctive sets of gatekeepers. Ushers, nurses, deaconesses, i.e., uniformed attendants with some designated title and role, are the gatekeepers of the static aspects of worship. Singers, preachers, and to some extent dancers are the gatekeepers of ecstatic worship, the people who "usher" the congregation into and out of the ecstatic state. Ushers attend to the physical movement of worshippers in and out of the sanctuary, and demarcate the temporal and spatial boundaries that encompass the sacred space. In other words, as ushers greet and seat each worshipper they are defining and managing the ritual space; their tenure of duty spans the entire worship time, from prelude to benediction. The preachers and singers direct the emotional and spiritual dynamics of the worship experience, and ushers participate in this process by attending to the special needs and security of persons experiencing the transition from static to ecstatic worship.

Since the ultimate objective of worship in the African-American Holiness and Pentecostal church tradition is some form of Spirit possession, the aesthetic and ethical norms that govern movement toward this objective are derived from the Bible and black culture. The distinctive songs, speech, and dances of these churches symbolically "usher" the saints "out" of this world and into a more authentic one discerned within sacred time and space.

There is a connection between the saints' rejection of "the world" and this world's rejection of the saints. The saints reject the world on the basis of biblically-derived ascetic commitments, i.e., the mandate to holiness; they are themselves "rejected" by the dominant host culture because of their race, sex, and class. When the saints sing "holy" unto the Lord, lift up holy hands, do the holy dance, in effect they are expressing their allegiance to a world where God has determined who is accepted and who will receive power. Moreover, their worship shows that they believe God is accepting of the praise, performances, and aesthetic standards that are characteristic of Africans in diaspora. The Holy Spirit has freed at least some of them from the pressure to conform to the worship styles of the dominant culture.

The saints are "in" a world that is sinful, oppressive, and discriminatory; they demonstrate that they are not "of" this world by purging themselves of its secularizing influences through rituals that meet their own criteria for cultural authenticity and biblical interpretation. In worship, the saints replicate the "other" world, the place where the oppressed outsider can be at home. Ethically, their allegiance to this "other" world requires them to be loving, honest, and pure, even in relation to their enemies. Just as the sanctuary or temple is the place of ritual possession, their bodies are temples of the Holy Spirit. Ritual purity in the sanctuary requires purity of body, mind, and spirit outside the sanctuary. By their worship the saints manifest the holy character of the God they serve; by clean living they demonstrate to the world that they possess the Spirit that possesses them in worship.

Questions to Ponder

1. Are you one of or at least identify with the many African-Americans and "pentecostals" who make up a significant sector of the Wesleyan/Holiness tradition? If you are or do, have you hoped to be better understood and appreciated by other believers who are not people of color or particularly expressive in their worship experiences? Do Christians unfairly stereotype each other's understanding and practice of holiness?

2. This author says that the underlying view of Holiness/Pentecostal worship is "being saved, sanctified, and filled with the Holy Ghost." Have you personally encountered this view in action? If so, what would you say about it positively and negatively?

3. A list of worship practices is identified as typical among African-American and Pentecostal holiness Christians. The ultimate goal of them is said to be some form of "Spirit possession." Is one on these practices new to you—and maybe worth introducing where you worship?

4. Might culture be more significant than race or ethnicity since this author reports that one finds both *fixed* and *fluid* worship patterns in "black Protestant churches." Some are said to be "lively" and some "quietistic," and some both. Is local culture also significant in

how Christian holiness is understood and practiced in any congregation?

5. Worship in African-American and Pentecostal congregations is said to be related significantly to both *this* world and the *other* world. Are both of these worlds prominent in the worship experiences you participate in from week to week? Should they be?

Chapter 17

Holiness and the Church:
Looking beyond Sectarianism

Barry L. Callen

Focus: It is typical to think of "sanctification" as an experience of transformation in the individual believer by the power of God's Spirit. But what about the church? The people of God struggle to be the body of Christ that God wants in this world. In the process, however, churches gather to themselves much that is so human, making them, to varying degrees, compromised witnesses of God's great grace. Some of the more "radical" holiness leaders of the nineteenth century became convinced that the church, as well as its members, needs to become holy. That meant the "visible" and not merely the "invisible" church. The world judges by what it actually sees. To the radical holiness visionaries, that meant that there should be an end to denominationalism, creedalism, and all "isms" that believers use to judge each other and divide from each other, thus distorting their common witness. Daniel S. Warner (1842–1895) was one of these radical visionaries. He took the Wesleyan "optimism of grace" to the corporate level of the church and in this way became idealistic about the comprehensiveness of the cleansing work of the Spirit. Thinking of "sectarianism" as the cutting into many pieces the Body of Christ, he cried out that God wanted a *holy* and thereby a *united* people functioning together on behalf of their common witness to the world.

During the decades in the United States following the Civil War, the Holiness Movement sought to be a reforming force *within* existing denominational structures. Many participants in this movement, however, and often reluctantly, became "separatists." That is, they judged themselves forced out of the their established denominational homes because of the commitment to holiness teaching. Various instances of such separations brought the accusation that those now on the "outside" were disrupters of church life. The supposed disrupters, however, insisted that they held a higher view of God's will for a holy and united church, one free of denominational dissention.

The Holiness Movement, one might say, was mainly "reformationist." Elements of it later became more "restorationist" based on early-church ideals they associated with the holiness emphasis. Daniel S. Warner and the Church of God movement (Anderson, Ind.) that he helped inspire were "separatists" who were seeking to stand clear of unnecessary divisions in church life. His motivation was anything but further dividing of the church by setting up another denomination based on anything human. As early as 1879, he chose to step outside not only the established churches, but soon even the relatively informal structures of the Holiness Movement that seemed insistent on supporting the legitimacy (or at least necessity) of denominations. Most holiness people focused on restoring holiness within their compromised denominations, not on questioning the legitimacy of the denominations themselves. Not so with Warner.

A Commission to Stand Free in the Spirit

Daniel Warner's "come-outism" was inspired by a vision of the church outside *all* denominations, enabled only by the experience of holiness and the dynamic of the Spirit's governance and gifting. He cared deeply about the unity of believers and saw holiness as the only way to it—one of the many hymns he composed is titled "The Bond of Perfectness." He judged that the continuing existence of multiple and often competitive denominational structures was an evil among God's people, one that God intended to end as the Bride was being prepared for Christ's soon return.

Warner and thousands of others "came out" in response to this vision of what was understood to be God's will for the sanctification of believers *and of the church itself.* Many holiness people felt themselves being "pushed out" of their denominational homes. Most of them would organize their own holiness church bodies. Warner determined to be an exception. His vision was rooted in the theological emphases of John Winebrenner (1797–1860), his "spiritual father."

Particular theological emphases had transformed Winebrenner's experience across the 1820s and led to the rupture of his relationship with the German Reformed Church in Pennsylvania. These emphases included:

1. The Bible is the Word of God, the only authoritative rule of faith and practice. This "only" left no place for church tradition, including human inventions like creeds, catechisms, rituals, etc.;

2. Spiritual regeneration, being born again, is necessary for a person to become a real Christian and thus a church member;

3. Regarding the church, the only requirement for membership in a local congregation is having been born again...."

Warner later fused these convictions with his experience of the unifying potential of Christian holiness. By 1880 he was ready to act against "sectarianism." An increasing number of leaders of the Holiness Movement were feeling significant tension between their passion for a holiness church renewal and the viability of continuance in their home denominations. Soon there would be new holiness-oriented denominations. That was one way of handling the coming together of holiness people.

Another way of searching for church order on the basis of Christian holiness was the more "radical" way of Warner. He became gripped by a "new commission" that he felt God had given to him. According to the March 7, 1878, entry in his personal journal: "The Lord showed me that holiness could never prosper upon sectarian soil encumbered by human creeds and party names, and he gave me a new commission *to join holiness and all truth together and build up the apostolic church of the living God."* Warner was seeking to apply the logic of Christian holiness, with all its perfectionist inclinations, to the integrity of church life and witness.

The Pivotal Holiness Convention

A convention of the Western Union Holiness Association convened in December, 1880, in Jacksonville, Illinois. Daniel Warner was to give a major address and was appointed to the program committee charged with planning the next convention. The topic of his address was "The Kind of Power Needed to Carry the Holiness Work." The main point he made was that "it is the power of God Himself that is needed for this work." He warned that "the devil is set against this work.... We need God's power to the fullest degree promised to meet this adversary."

Some comments of others at this convention disturbed Warner. For instance, Thomas Doty from Cleveland, Ohio, said that "if you belong to a church, it is your duty to promote holiness right in it: in the Presbyterian church, as a Presbyterian; in the Baptist church, as a Baptist, etc." Doty admitted that he disliked the whole denominational idea, but God "permits it, and so must we." M. L. Haney (a Methodist Episcopal leader) attacked come-outers "who insist on the silly dogma of no-churchism, and favor the disorganization of all Christian forces." This convention was a setting where denominationalism was being supported and membership in a denomination even made a requirement of continued fellowship in the holiness organization. Surely, thought Warner, Doty was wrong about God supporting the status-quo assumption of the acceptability of rampant division of Christ's body, the church. Maybe being a "come-outer" was the way to go. Warner saw the charge of no-churchism as an unfair demeaning of the unifying potential of the promised sanctifying power of the Spirit.

Warner believed deeply in the church and refused to accept the claim that genuine reliance on the Holy Spirit to establish and guide the church is inevitably the way of anarchy. Is God the author of confusion? Warner was now done with the business-as-usual way of denominational religion. He had the elements of a rationale for a new and more radical holiness movement, one intending to be truly trans-denominational in the sanctifying and unifying power of the Spirit of

God. Now joined in his mind and heart were the passion for Christian holiness, the dream of Christian unity, and the belief that the first enables the second, but only when free of the artificial restrictions of humans attempting to organize and "run" church life. Human hands must be taken off of God's church!

The remainder of Warner's life and ministry was devoted to restoring the unity of God's people through the sanctifying work of the Holy Spirit. He was a "come-outer." He and many others "saw the church," a vision of the seamless, undivided, truly holy body of Christ. He proclaimed that the "perfect love" of sanctification enables Christians to live above sin, including the sin of rending the body of Christ. Human lines of denomination, race, sex, and social status were to be abandoned in the face of the transforming grace of God in Christ through the Spirit. The vision called for refusing to erect or honor as legitimate any human controls on Christian fellowship. The church is a "pentecostal" fellowship. God the Spirit sets the members in the church and gifts them with divine gifts for its proper functioning. The Bible is the only creed. It's God's church! The church exists for mission, and disunity is hurtful to the church's attempt to bear a credible witness in the world. Barry L. Callen's biography of Daniel Warner is titled *It's God's Church!*

The Continuing Vision

The ministries of Daniel Warner and the many others with him resulted in what now is the Church of God movement (Anderson). One of its historians, John W. V. Smith, offered six propositions about the relationship between holiness and church unity. They reflect Warner's "new commission" and, in Smith's view, remain worthy of careful consideration (*Wesleyan Theological Journal*, Spring, 1975). They are:

1. Believers in holiness must not be too ready to accept easy answers in rationalizing division in the church. Even "liberal" Christians pray God's forgiveness for participating in the sin of division.

2. A passionate concern for personal sanctification should not subvert an equally great concern for the doctrine of the church. It is well to

keep in mind that the Apostle Paul used the word *sanctify* in regard to *both* persons and the church.

3. In the light of Christ's prayer for the church (Jn. 17), the concepts of "spiritual unity" and "invisible oneness" are inadequate and inconsistent with the apparent implications of "perfect love."

4. Associationalism and conciliarism are abortive approaches to Christian unity in that they only mitigate the evils of division and do not remove them.

5. Non-denominationalism is an inadequate concept for the full realization of Christian unity in that it expresses primarily a negative rather than a positive character of the church.

6. This time in Christian history seems to be an especially propitious one for all proponents of holiness to dedicate themselves to giving major attention to the relational implications of holiness doctrine. Under the leadership of the Holy Spirit, holy Christians may be able to lead the way toward unification of the whole church in order that the world may believe.

There is a divine vision here worthy of careful consideration. How can the church become more "apostolic," "catholic," and "holy" in our day?

Questions to Ponder

1. Is denominationalism a necessity in church life? Is it an evil even if a sad necessity? Is any alternative to the many denominations an unrealistic dream and merely an invitation to anarchy?

2. Think again about the prayer of Jesus (Jn. 17) for the unity of his disciples for the sake of their mission and witness in the world. Should Christian holiness be thought of as crucial for the individual believer *and* for the healing of the church itself?

3. Some hymn lyrics written by Daniel Warner are titled "The Bond of Perfectness," a beloved song in the tradition of the Church of God movement (Anderson). Is the "perfectness," the power of holy

love, the only bond that can bring unity to the divided people of God?

4. Church historian John W. V. Smith says that "associatonalism" and "conciliarism" are abortive approaches to Christian unity. Such approaches were tried many times across the twentieth century, admittedly with mixed success. Are there better alternatives? See the next chapter by John Smith and Gilbert Stafford.

5. What has become very common today is a weakening of the traditional denominations and the dramatic growth of congregations that are "independent" or "non-denominational." Does this bring Christian unity or increase anarchy? Is the experience of truly transformed lives (holiness) the one thing that can truly unify believers?

Chapter 18

Holiness and Unity: Fulfilling the Prayers of Jesus

John W. V. Smith and
Gilbert W. Stafford

Focus: The Holiness Movement in the United States sought to bring fresh spiritual life back into many individual believers and, through them, reinvigorate the church structures with which they were affiliated. This movement's agenda has not featured a primary concern about the organizational disunity of Christians. In fact, many holiness people, in their enthusiasm and occasional narrowness, have furthered the disunity of believers with their own new denominations. Jesus prayed for both the holiness and unity of his disciples (Jn. 17). Can holiness unite instead of divide? Should holiness people stand clear of or join in the efforts of non-holiness believers to achieve greater Christian unity? John Smith affirms the unifying potential of holiness, and his colleague Gilbert Stafford calls for the bold involvement of holiness people with other believers in efforts designed to fulfill the prayer of our Lord.

There are two affirmations about the church, the body of Christ on earth, on which almost all Christians would be agreed: (1) God's church is one; (2) God's church is holy. To question these statements would be to contradict the expressed wishes of our Lord in John 17, to disregard the churchly metaphors of the Apostle Paul, and to ignore declarations about the church by most of the other New Testament writers. So, when any follower of Christ announces that he or she believes in the unity and sanctity of the church, that person creates little excitement, evokes almost no argument, and finds few challengers. We all accept these ideals, and even the most ardent non-creedalist can heartily avow, "I believe in the one, holy, catholic Church."

Once the affirmations are made, however, there comes the added task of elaborating their meaning and bringing that meaning to present reality. Here the complications and difficulties begin—and go on and on and on. The problem is perhaps best identified and simplified in the reported conversation between two sectarians in which one sarcastically said to the other, "After all, when we get down to basics, each of us is earnestly striving to do the will of the Lord, you in your way and I in God's!" The result, as we all know, is a severely fractured "body of Christ," a blemished "bride" with spots and wrinkles and other such things, and multiple "buildings" made with human hands.

Holiness is a Key to Unity

We need not elaborate the sadly divided state of Christendom. It is obvious to everyone. We are all too well aware of the hundreds of sects and denominations, parties, camps, wings, factions, and "isms" that cluster under separate labels and banners. We also recognize the fact that most Christians are neither repentant nor apologetic about these distinctions. Indeed, they are not only willing but proud to wear a nametag that separates them from other Christians and, in effect, says, "Thank God, I'm not as others are!"

Yet, in the context of such universal acceptance of the ideal of Christian unity, there is a certain discomfort about this separateness. This is not a recent development. Uneasiness about division in the church goes all the way back to the first century. Much of the development of creeds and structures in the primitive and medieval periods of Christian history were specifically aimed at solving the problem of disunity. The sixteenth-century Reformers were not unmindful of the charge that, in separating from the Roman Catholic Church, they were guilty of schism. In order to live with their own consciences, both Luther and Calvin were compelled to develop their own internal rationale for separating from Catholicism. Christian holiness leaders in more recent times generally have tended to give only marginal attention to the matter of Christian unity. They have steadfastly defended the denominational system and disclaimed "come-outism" as extreme and unnecessary.

The fact that holiness people have been strongly associational does not mean that they have been particularly concerned about the problems of Christian disunity. Their cooperation has been focused on a specific purpose—the promotion of holiness—and has not been directed toward the overcoming of division and the unification of the church. Some holiness leaders have regarded sectism as "sin," have looked to "perfect love" as the only escape from division in the church, and have envisioned Christian unity as a visible fellowship of all the "saints" (see the previous chapter on Daniel Warner). Believers in holiness must not be too ready to accept easy answers in rationalizing division in the church. Even "liberal" Christians pray God's forgiveness for participating in the sin of division.

A passionate concern for personal sanctification should not subvert an equally great concern for the doctrine of the church. It is well to keep in mind that the Apostle Paul uses the word sanctify in regard to both persons and the church. In the light of Christ's prayer for the Church (Jn. 17), the concepts of "spiritual unity" and "invisible oneness" are inadequate and inconsistent with the intended implications of "perfect love." This time in Christian history seems to be an especially propitious one for all proponents of holiness to dedicate themselves to giving major attention to the relational implications of this doctrine. The goal is that, under the leadership of the Holy Spirit, we may be able to lead the way toward unification of the whole church so that, indeed, the world may believe.

Practicing Holiness with Believers of Other Christian Traditions

The first World Conference on Faith and Order was held in Lausanne, Switzerland, in 1927. There were 394 delegates representing 108 church bodies from around the world. The first participation of holiness leaders was at Montreal in 1963 with a delegate (Gene W. Newberry) and two observers (Louis Meyer and John W. V. Smith) from the Church of God movement (Anderson), and with two U.S.A. delegates from the Salvation Army (Commissioner S. Hepburn and Lt.-Col. P. S. Kaiser). Faith and Order work in the United States is now sponsored by the National Council of the Churches of Christ in the U.S.A. (NCCC). In keeping with the long-standing tradition of including churches that are not members of the NCCC, present membership encompasses a wide range of churches. The Wesleyan Theological Society has long been active in such "ecumenical" affairs.

The Benefits of Participation

Since many conservative Christians oppose conciliar efforts to enhance Christian unity, one question is obvious. What, if any, are the benefits of such participation? I [Gilbert Stafford] will choose Faith and Order since it seeks greater cooperation and unity and I have considerable personal experience with it. Participation in this ongoing unity effort by those from various holiness traditions has been very limited. I list the following nine points, hoping that being aware of these values of participation will encourage greater involvement and less suspicion by leaders of the Wesleyan/Holiness/Pentecostal traditions.

1. Participation is an opportunity to learn *about* other traditions in a dialogical setting.

2. Faith and Order is an opportunity to learn *from* other traditions.

3. Faith and Order provides an arena of discussion with a wide spectrum of Christian traditions.

4. Faith and Order provides each participant the opportunity to teach other traditions about one's own tradition.

5. Faith and Order work is the opportunity for one's own tradition to recognize in other traditions dimensions of the apostolic faith which lie dormant in one's own.

6. Faith and Order is the opportunity to develop a deeper understanding and appreciation of one's own tradition.

7. Faith and Order work is the opportunity for churches to guard against becoming root bound within their own narrower tradition.

8. Faith and Order is the opportunity for a wide spectrum of ecclesial bodies to work together in theological endeavors.

9. Faith and Order provides the opportunity for us to become interpreters of other traditions at points where they may be misunderstood.

As a representative of the holiness tradition of contemporary Christianity, I wish to be clear. The Faith and Order movement is certainly no panacea for the dividedness of Christ's church, but it is an opportunity for that dividedness to be addressed within the context of a broad spectrum of Christian faith traditions. Many have been the times when I have been thoroughly frustrated in the meetings and by the process. There have been times when I have wondered whether it was worthwhile. But the benefits far outweigh the liabilities.

At Faith and Order meetings (twice a year), I often desire the participation of more of my holiness colleagues in the faith. By participating, a church has much to gain. Not only may it feed into the bloodstream of the wider Christian community its own treasures of the apostolic faith, but also it can be immeasurably enriched by the treasures of the same faith which others feed into the bloodstream. But of greatest importance is this: Faith and Order is one additional small step toward the fulfillment of our Lord's prayer in John 17:21–22 that we "may all be one," to the end "that the world may believe." It is one additional even if limited attempt toward responding positively to Paul's plea in Ephesians 4:1–3 for us "to lead a life worthy of the calling to which [we] . . . have been called . . . making every effort to maintain the unity of the Spirit in the bond of peace."

Questions to Ponder

1. Have you heard of the "ecumenical movement"? It is a worldwide effort of numerous church bodies to increase awareness of each other and enhance Christian witness and service together. Is your particular church body active in some part of this movement? Should it be?

2. Does your church body feel confident that its beliefs and practices are closer to God's will than those of other denominations? Are divisive attitudes alive and well? Are they hurtful to the church's witness to the world?

3. Gilbert Stafford vigorously counters all condescending attitudes among Christians with his list of values found in cooperative church dialogue. Can you really learn from believers in other Christian traditions? Are you open to such learning, or is such involvement mostly an invitation to "compromise" of the truth you already know?

4. John Smith reports that the promotion of holiness has been focused mostly on transforming individuals and revitalizing denominations. But he argues that holiness also has the potential of melting divisive church divisions. Is "sectism" really a sin? If so, is holiness the answer? Is there some setting in your community where believers are coming together from various denominations for the benefit of all? How could you get more involved?

5. Have you heard of the Wesleyan Holiness Consortium? It is championing today the power of holiness to bring together many pastors, lay leaders, and denominational heads to enhance a united witness for Christ. Go to this web site to learn more: www.holinessandunity.org.

Chapter 19

Holiness and World Christianity: Mission in "Foreign" Cultures

DAVID BUNDY

Focus: The Holiness Movement is often thought of as primarily a nineteenth-century development in the United States. In fact, it has a very long history and continues to this day, having important representatives in many countries of the world. These representatives, although sometimes rooted deeply in their own places and cultures, unfortunately are viewed frequently by American holiness people as all the results of the mission efforts of North Americans. But Christian holiness is an important reality not limited to time, place, culture, or Western mission. Many holiness churches and movements worldwide have not grown directly from Western mission efforts, and often they are not even known by American holiness people. Nor does the experience of holiness bring a pre-set pattern of views and practices on all subjects. In fact, the Wesleyan/Holiness movements of the world have been diverse since their beginnings. All theologies, including holiness theologies, are shaped in part by their locations and cultures of origin. David Bundy explores aspects of the worldwide holiness movements through his review of a book by Howard A. Snyder and an important article of his own.

Howard A. Snyder has been living and thinking about Christian mission for a long time. He has informed and provoked readers with an extensive list of well-received books. *Global Good News* (2001), for instance, is an important book he edited that brings together some of his thoughts as well as those of a network of prominent mission colleagues. Most of these colleagues have had significant intercultural experience. The book demands the attention of all Christians, especially Wesleyan/Holiness people concerned about the church, mission, and evangelism. It is an engaging and well-edited book. The authors wrestle with the issues of Christian mission. Their essays reflect both a diversity of perspective and a common theme. It is that Christians have too often handicapped the "good news" by limiting the gospel of Jesus to particular cultural and intellectual structures.

During the last four decades, "post-modern" philosophy has enabled much of the world to value its own experiences and understand the limits of its own cultures. Any version of Christianity's claim to be a global religion with a single definition has been called into question. This global awareness of cultural diversity has complicated the task of mission in other cultures and in one's own. The book edited by Howard Snyder responds to this problem in two ways. First, it affirms that the diversity of the church can enrich the diverse elements of the church and make churches more welcoming. Second, in the words of Snyder, "properly understood and incarnated, the gospel of Jesus Christ really is global good news. It is the best possible good news for the whole cosmos and for every person and culture in it" (235).

What does this mean for the Wesleyan/Holiness movements? They have been diverse since their beginnings. From the time of John Wesley's mission to Georgia and Thomas Coke's missions to the Caribbean, Nova Scotia, Ghana, and India, the Wesleyan tradition has been diverse. The American experiences of Wesleyan evangelism, from the days of Lorenzo Dow and Francis Asbury, have brought a rich diversity into the Wesleyan fold. The Wesleyan/Holiness movements that swept through the other churches and then grew alienated from the Methodists reached diverse European ethnic groups and people from different racial backgrounds. Mission work only extended the diversity.

A large percentage of Methodists live outside North America and Europe. The same is the case for Holiness believers. The immigration processes of the last half-century have brought thousands of Dominican, Haitian, Brazilian, Ugandan, Tanzanian, Japanese, Indian, and other Holiness believers to North America. The churches need to find ways to help these diverse Holiness people prosper in their new cultural contexts. They will also need to identify holiness themes from these diverse communities of faith, themes that they want to communicate in mission and evangelism across generational lines. They will need to find what they can offer to others as an understanding of Christian faith and then decide if they can open their doors to those outside. They will need to make the Holiness churches, all of them, the bearers of a multi-cultural "good news."

****

There is a crucial problem when researching the global structures of the holiness movements in Christianity worldwide. It is that holiness churches have had to work with the conceptual framework of what scholars have considered "holiness." But is "holiness" limited to the nineteenth-century North American definition and sets of personal relationships of the National Camp-Meeting Association? Must one first have to be a Methodist before one can be "holiness"? A Holiness scholar recently observed that all "Holiness" people were related to the nineteenth-century American camp meeting tradition and to a version of Methodism. I argue that such a definition is untenable, even in North America, and that the reality of "holiness" churches around the world, both past and present, requires a serious revisiting of the historical definitions of holiness ecumenism and theology.

In North America, the present Holiness churches are so separated that they scarcely recognize each other in meaningful ways. Rarely do scholars not related to the larger European-American Holiness churches attend the Wesleyan Theological Society. There are few, if any, sustained WTS connections to Holiness scholars outside North America. Holiness believers in non-Holiness churches are even farther removed from conversation, much less cooperation. As well. There also are the continuing results of the North American experience of the Pentecostal revival of 1906 and following. Holiness Pentecostals in North America are separated from their Holiness brothers and sisters even more than they are from their Pentecostal colleagues. It remains to be seen whether the recent joint meetings of the Society for Pentecostal Studies and the Wesleyan Theological Society will bring these related traditions closer together. This effort is helpful.

Because of these divides (and others), the Holiness movements outside North America have often been defined as, and limited to, the history of the missionary efforts of the North American Holiness churches. This is very limiting since most of these churches had small numbers of missionaries before World War II. It does not provide a basis for interpreting the religious (holiness) reality experienced by Africans, Asians, Australians, and Latin Americans.

Historians outside of North America have been hampered in their analysis of the influence of the holiness movements by the North American definition of "holiness" and the lack of meaningful access to North American and European sources. We should be aware that understandings of sanctification and the holy life are significantly different in various countries.

Evolving of Multiple Holiness Traditions

All theologies, not just Christian theologies, are shaped by their contexts. The mission movement that dominated Anglo-American religion during the nineteenth century developed particular forms and approaches. Wesleyan/Holiness mission was, from the beginning, trans-Atlantic and reached beyond the boundaries of Methodism. The primary activists of the nineteenth century were Lorenzo Dow, William Taylor, James Hudson Taylor, and the Booth family. William Taylor was influential in establishing Holiness Methodist congregations and inspiring Holiness and Pentecostal denominations around the world. His mission theory was adapted by the Scandinavian Pentecostal movements and has had a major role in defining what it means, missionally, structurally, and theologically, to be Holiness and/or Pentecostal outside North America.

The acceptance, adaptation, and retransmission of the Holiness ideals in Europe are just beginning to be understood. There were trans-Atlantic revivalist efforts by Lorenzo Dow, James Caughey, Phoebe Palmer, William Taylor, D. L. Moody, Robert Pearsall Smith, Asa Mahan, and others, including missionaries of the Methodist Episcopal, Evangelical and United Brethren, Anglican, Baptist, and Presbyterian traditions. In England, Holiness revivalism, as well as Keswick and the Salvation Army, effected social and institutional changes. In Germany and Sweden, the tradition produced institutions and denominations as well as changes among the Lutherans and Methodists. In Sweden, the Baptist Union (and other denominations) was heavily influenced by the trans-Atlantic Holiness connections.

The influence of the Holiness movements was extensive and enduring in Denmark. In other areas, such as France, Switzerland, the Netherlands and Belgium, the Holiness influence was more subtle, but clearly present and to this date inadequately analyzed. In the global context, the Holiness tradition is represented around the world by the Salvation Army as well as by both indigenous movements and mission churches related to the North American churches. Often, the non-North American daughter churches have out-evangelized and out-grown the parent churches. This is true for the Free Methodists, the Missionary Church, Wesleyans, the Church of God (Anderson), the Church of God (Cleveland), and the Church of God of Prophecy.

The preliminary result of tracing the evolution of the many holiness traditions and revivals (non-institutionalized traditions) is to become aware of a vast network of diverse groups of Christian holiness persons and churches. These holiness networks have waxed and waned, and then flourished again in a variety of cultural contexts, under diverse leadership, and with varying degrees of awareness of the other networks, or even of their own. The search for what the holiness movements have in common needs to include detailed historical, sociological, and cultural analyses of these diverse and interwoven networks within and across cultural structures.

For example, oral interviews have suggested to me that to be in the Salvation Army in the Netherlands or in Norway is very different from being in the Army in London or in the U.S.A. The uniform is the same, but the spiritualities, competitive sources of theological reflection, and understandings of holiness are quite different. A scholarly and worldwide study of unity and diversity in the Salvation Army would make a distinct contribution to the understanding of the evolution of holiness traditions in different cultures.

Local church leaders of the mission churches of various holiness denominations around the world have spoken to me of a particular frustration. They are experiencing being tied closely to policies made by people who have large offices in buildings in their countries built with North American funds. However, the leaders who sit in these offices sometimes have minimal understanding of the cultures within which they are temporarily living and seeking to serve. They, in turn, must report to people who have even less understanding of the larger world. If these mission churches were allowed to meaningfully interact with their own cultural contexts and control their own educational structures, they might enrich the mother churches as well as the other holiness churches present around the world.

The question of the "death of the Holiness movement" has been the subject of considerable discussion in scholarly and popular Holiness circles. From the perspective of isolated North American denominational or para-church perspectives, that may appear true. If, however, one looks at the diversity and vitality of Holiness networks around the world over the last two centuries, it would appear that the Holiness networks are very much alive and well! In addition, it would appear that holiness history, theology, and mission are more complicated than has generally been thought, and so very much more interesting!

Questions to Ponder

1. Western Europeans and North Americans have had a tendency to define holiness theology, practice, and people in relation to themselves and their own histories and mission efforts. What have been the results? Is the holiness world mostly the outcome of North American missions?

2. David Bundy identifies a serious problem. He says that holiness scholars and churches have minimal significant contact with each other, and certainly with holiness bodies outside North America and Western Europe. This separation, often merely caused by de-

fault, is even greater between holiness and pentecostal bodies, many of which have common holiness roots. What can and should be done about this?

3. Do you agree that theology and religious practice are shaped significantly by the particular cultural context in which they arise? If they are, is all truth relative, dependent on circumstances? Given growing awareness of the many diversities in our world, should this question be addressed seriously?

4. Recall the report about mission executives being quite out of touch culturally with the area in which they seek to administer holiness programs and people. Should leaders closer to the local culture be given more authority in such matters? Is the same situation present in your denomination, with national leaders seeming to be out of touch with local matters over which they have some authority? Is this inevitable?

5. Has the holiness movement "died"? Is it alive where you worship? Might it be alive far from where you are, and, if so, are you aware of it? Do you agree with David Bundy that diversity brings its complications and great interest?

Chapter 20

Holiness and End Times: An Optimism of Grace

MICHAEL E. LODAHL

Focus: The word "eschatology" must be understood. It is the Christian study of destiny and fulfillment, not merely of the events leading to the end of history—as many people treat the subject. You can see from the title of Michael Lodahl's original article (see detail at end) that he is cautious about being overly enthusiastic when it comes to predicting and claiming detailed knowledge of "final things." Lodahl is reflecting a caution shared by John Wesley, and by Jesus long before him. Jesus deflected the curiosity questions of his disciples in the direction of present responsibilities. Wesley was concerned that a preoccupation with the future tends to undermine the present quest for "Christian perfection." So, here is the key question. Is the Christian hope best implemented by focus on history's end and beyond or on the potential impact of God's grace on the here and now? In this chapter, the present wins out.

In one of the classes I teach annually, my students and I study John Wesley's book *A Plain Account of Christian Perfection*. The repeated reading of this fascinating little volume has had the effect of pushing a certain question to the surface of my thinking. Why did Wesley show so little sympathy and have so little patience with eschatological (end times) fervor, which he tended to identify with "enthusiasm"? He does not tell us precisely on what grounds he opposed these enthusiasts or why he was so adamant about his denying the validity of their end-time predictions.

Undoubtedly one reason for his opposition was the pastoral motivation of desiring to avoid the unpleasant task of having to "pick up the pieces" of shattered hopes, and even faith, after a failed prediction. There is another, a holiness-oriented reason. At the end of Wesley's little book we find a theological clue. Wesley had determined that these end-time enthusiasts stimulated opposition to "Christian perfection." He tended to dismiss speculation, especially as it touches on sensationalistic matters, as being unimportant, even hurtful in that it occupies the mind with issues not rooted in salvation.

How different is the constant speculation that comes from our modern-day religious futurists, ranging from the traveling evangelists with their detailed charts to the Hal Lindseys, all of whom trade on human curiosity and fear by their end-time scenarios? The fact is that they encourage their hearers to concentrate on reserving a place in a future age. Wesley taught a different attitude, one which is concerned that preoccupation with end-times may cloud the issues central to salvation. His approach tends to encourage us to do what we can to *serve* the present age, indeed to *preserve* it, rather than to flee from it and expect/hope for its soon demise. Suspicions against traditional "eschatological" fervor, therefore, are inherent in Wesley's understanding of the divine-human relationship. They also should be inherent in our understandings.

Perfecting Grace in This Life

The place to begin is with the recognition that eschatology is, in fact, at the very heart of Wesley's doctrine of entire sanctification. To be sure, it is a *realizable* eschatology since Wesley insists that it is possible *in this life* to be brought to a perfection of love for God and neighbor. By differing with those who taught that Christian perfection occurs only at the point of or after death, and by holding out for the possibilities of divine grace to perfect us in love in this life, Wesley was making room for an eschatological hope that could become more than a hope, but rather a gracious reality in the here and now.

The Wesleyan insistence on the possibility of entire sanctification in this life testifies not only to the transforming power of God's love and grace, but also to the potential of this present world becoming an arena of authentic goodness and love, or what the Hebrew prophets called *shalom*. One might even surmise that the same impatience Wesley showed toward those who testified of being in the "state" of perfection, because they tended to rest in a past experience, he might extend toward those who tend to look ahead to some future moment of eschatological perfection. For Wesley, now is to be the day of full salvation. He was impatient with focus on the past or future since they both obscure the present possibilities of sanctifying grace and human responsibility.

To the extent that eschatology concerns itself with what God is going to do to put an end to history, specifically in the coming again of our Lord Jesus Christ, then in a sense we do believe that God will "save us without ourselves." And to an extent, many traditional eschatological scenarios either imply or encourage a certain hopelessness about the project of history. Do they not to that extent mitigate against Wesley's doctrine of Christian perfection as a *realizable* eschatology? What if the real "end" of history is the gracious (re)creation of human beings to become, in this life, lovers of God and neighbor? Are we not to hope that holiness experienced in the heart and implemented in the world should and can be now?

The pattern of divine activity that Wesley finds in human experience, God's general manner of working, is that of gracious assistance, not force. It is an enlightening and strengthening of human understanding and affections, not their deletion or destruction. This gracious synergism provided Wesley with a model not simply for divine-human interaction, but for the entirety of the God-world interaction. God could and would work cooperatively with us humans in the transformation of this troubled world. Writing out of this optimism of grace, Wesley predicts the triumphal spread of the gospel from one nation and people to another as God gradually renews the face of the earth until the vision of the Revelator is fulfilled and "the Lord God omnipotent reigneth!"

Persuasion and Enablement

Today we tend not to share Wesley's naive-sounding optimism, but do we have good reason to reject his interpretation of God's mode of activity as persuasion and gracious enablement, in contrast to a unilateral, manipulative, apocalyptic in-breaking of history? Is it consistent or coherent to insist on synergism at the level of individual spiritual experience and yet hold to an eschatological hope of unilateral divine intrusion on the historical or cosmic level?

The Wesleyan message of perfect love for God and neighbor *in this life* provides an optimism about the possibilities of grace in human existence, societies, and history that belies any disabling despair. The fact that, for Wesley, Jesus is the great model and exemplar of such love supports my contention that what God reveals to us in Christ, both about God and about ourselves, is a direct challenge to future scenarios that write off history as hopeless. The synergism of grace underlying Wesley's doctrine of Christian perfection points to the validity and importance of history. God cares about the *now*!

I argue that a thoroughly Wesleyan eschatology does posit an "end" for creation and history, but in a particular sense. God's end is that human beings, those creatures fashioned to image God, and thus to be God's representatives in the world and in history, would join God in covenantal relationship and cooperation toward the redemption and healing of creation. God's creative activity is an ongoing task. While humanity as a whole has not thus far done an effective job of contributing to the wellness or *shalom* of creation, there is no reason to assume that God is ready to give up on the project of the covenantal freedom and the responsibility of human beings.

The Genesis doctrine of creation, including re-creation in the flood narrative, is a profound affirmation of God's underlying predisposition toward maintaining the possibilities of adventurous relationship with this created order. Such an understanding of creation goes hand-in-hand with Wesley's optimism of grace, which insists that it is possible in this life (and hence, in this world and during our history) to love God and neighbor with all one's being. If such love is possible for one, it is in principle possible, by God's transforming, empowering grace, for all. Hence, individuals and societies, graced and enabled by God's presence, can yet move, at least in principle, toward the divine vision of *shalom.* Eschatology traditionally tends to focus on closure, on God finally saying "Enough!" to the project of creaturely otherness and freedom. The Wesleyan/Holiness/Pentecostal traditions want to keep the present alive, hopeful, and meaningful in the meantime.

This perspective has obvious implications for developing a Christian, and particularly a Wesleyan commitment to social and economic justice, as well as to the ecological health of the planet. Good stewardship by humans of the created order is stewardship for the long haul! One might ask whether the purpose of God's venture in creating is aborted by eschatological scenarios in which human activity and responsibility are brought to closure.

Even if our Creator truly is committed to the venture and risk of freedom exercised by the creature, there is no guarantee that this grand "experiment" will end satisfactorily. While the grace of God's presence in human life and societies is faithful and true (Ps. 146:6–9), that grace is persuasive rather than coercive. The great majority of eschatological scenarios that Christians have envisioned are coercive in nature. God lures rather than forces things to be as they are intended.

Perhaps the Wesleyan view is wrapped up in the theme of eschatological love as addressed in 1 John, which was of paramount importance for Wesley: "By this, love is perfected with us, that we may have confidence in the day of judgment; . . . there is no fear in love, but perfect love casts out fear, because fear involves punishment, and the one who fears is not perfected in love. We love, because He first loved us" (4:17–19). Such love is possible only in the atmosphere of authentic freedom. Moreover, such love is also the deepest meaning and fulfillment, or end, of human freedom.

Such perspective sheds light, I think, on the concluding sentence of Wesley's sermon "The New Creation." It reads: "And, to crown all, there will be a deep, an intimate, an uninterrupted union with God; a constant communion with the Father and his Son Jesus Christ, through the Spirit; a continual enjoyment of the Three-One God, and of all the creatures in him!"

Keynotes of a Wesleyan Orientation

By taking such an approach to eschatology, one can see the following as key to a Wesleyan orientation:

1. The Wesleyan proclamation is that it is possible by divine grace to love God and neighbor perfectly in this life. This, particularly when joined with the Genesis affirmation of this world and this life as God's arena of covenantal faithfulness, ought to energize and embolden believers. A commitment to the Wesleyan theological tradition brings focus to God's goal, God's intended end for creation. It is the transformation of this present age through universal love.

2. Because Scripture envisions a new heaven and new earth, the Wesleyan tradition's commitment to the idea of gracious synergism within the context of divinely ordained "otherness" is not necessarily dependent on the survival of the present universe.

3. On the other hand, whatever eschatological fulfillment of creation Wesleyans might envision is only coherent and consistent with the first two points if it upholds an eschatological perfection of love, which seems inevitably to imply a continuing situation of glorious freedom and responsibility.

4. And thus we pray, as Jesus taught his disciples, "May your reign arrive; may your will be done *on earth* as it is in heaven." Amen!

Questions to Ponder

1. Have you ever been in the position of having to "pick up the pieces" of shattered hopes and even faith when a predicted end-time event has failed to materialize? Christian church history is littered with failures to predict accurately the future of God. Why do believers tend to keep making such predictions, and insisting that they are assured biblical truth?

2. Do you agree that the speculators trade on people's curiosity and fear? Jesus did quite the opposite. See the Wesleyan-oriented book *Faithful in the Meantime* by Barry L. Callen (1997) for a good presentation of a proper approach to Christian eschatology.

3. John Wesley is said to have resisted end-time speculations in favor of a "realized eschatology," one supportive of the goal of perfect love *in this life*. Is the meaning of this clear to you? Read again what Michael Lodahl says here and try putting it in your own words. Has this world gotten so bad that only the return of Christ can launch its transformation?

4. What are the tenses of Christian life? Is it proper to say that the past is foundation, the future is destiny, and the present is the time for mission and an optimism about what God through us can accomplish in the meantime? Is the goal of Christian holiness not to focus of the "perfecting" of the here and now?

5. Note Lodahl's explanation of a cooperative "synergism" as God's chosen and typical way of working out his will in this world. Is the meaning of this clear to you? For a further discussion of this, see Barry L. Callen's article in the *Wesleyan Theological Journal* titled "Soteriological Synergism and Its Surrounding Seductions," 46:2 (Fall 2011). God is a covenant-making Lord who chooses to persuade rather than coerce, to enhance partners instead of manufacture marionettes.

Editors, Contributors, and Original Articles

David D. Bundy, Th.D. (Uppsala University), former Associate Provost for Library and Information Technology and Associate Professor of History at Fuller Theological Seminary, currently Research Professor of World Christian Studies, New York Theological Seminary. He served as President of the Wesleyan Theological Society. Bundy's book review in Chapter 19 is about the 2001 book edited by Howard A. Snyder and titled *Global Good News: Mission in a New Context*. Bundy's article, the second portion of Chapter 19, is titled "The Holiness Movements in World Christianity: Historiographical Questions." It appeared in the *Wesleyan Theological Journal*, vol. 38:1 (Spring 2003). Used by permission.

Barry L. Callen, D.Rel. (Chicago Theological Seminary) and Ed.D. (Indiana University), is University Professor Emeritus of Christian Studies at Anderson University, where he also served as Dean of Anderson School of Theology and Vice-President for Academic  Affairs. Callen serves as Editor of the *Wesleyan Theological Journal*, Aldersgate Press, and Anderson University Press, and is a winner of the Lifetime Achievement Award granted by the Wesleyan Theological Society. The original article in Chapter 17 by Barry L. Callen is titled "Daniel Sydney Warner: Joining Holiness and All Truth." It appeared in the *Wesleyan Theological Journal*, vol. 30:1 (Spring 1995). Used by permission. Dr. Callen is co-editor of this present volume.

Allan Coppedge, Ph.D. (University of Cambridge), was Beeson Professor of Christian Theology at Asbury Theological Seminary. The original article in Chapter 18 by Allan Coppedge was entitled "Holiness and Discipleship." It appeared in the *Wesleyan Theological Journal*, vol. 15:2 (Spring 1980). Used by permission.

Kenneth E. Geiger, D.D. (Asbury Theological Seminary), was elected general superintendent of the former United Missionary Church, and later was elected the first president of the Missionary Church. Geiger also served as the president of the National Holiness Association, and helped found the Wesleyan Theological Society. The original article in Chapter 3 by Kenneth E. Geiger was entitled "Biblical Basis of Holiness." It appeared in the *Wesleyan Theological Journal*, vol. 1.1 (1966). Used by permission.

Henry H. Knight III, Ph.D. (Emory University), is the Donald and Pearl Wright Professor of Wesleyan Studies at Saint Paul School of Theology. He served as President of the Wesleyan Theological Society. Henry Knight's original article in Chapter 15 is titled "Worship and Sanctification." This article appeared in the *Wesleyan Theological Journal*, vol. 32:2 (Fall 1997). Used by permission.

Harold B. Kuhn, Ph.D. (Harvard University), was Professor of Philosophy and Chair of the Division of Theology and Philosophy of Religion at Asbury Theological Seminary. Harold Kuhn's original article in Chapter 10 is titled "Burning Issues in the Life of Sanctity." It appeared in the *Wesleyan Theological Journal*, vol. 3 (1968). Used by permission.

Diane Leclerc, Ph.D. (Drew University), is Professor of Historical Theology at Northwest Nazarene University. She served as President of the Wesleyan Theological Society, and won the Smith/Wynkoop Book Award. Diane Leclerc's original article in Chapter 10 is titled "Holiness and Power: Toward a Wesleyan Theology of Dis-Ability." It appeared in the *Wesleyan Theological Journal*, vol. 44:1 (Spring 2009). Used by permission.

Michael E. Lodahl, Ph.D. (Emory University), is Professor of Theology and World Religions at Point Loma Nazarene University. He served as President of the Wesleyan Theological Society. The original article in Chapter 20 by Michael Lodahl is titled "Wesleyan Reservations About Eschatological 'Enthusiasm'." It appeared in the *Wesleyan Theological Journal*, vol. 29:1-21 (Spring-Fall 1994). Used by permission.

Mark A. Maddix, Ph.D. (Trinity Evangelical Divinity School), is Professor of Practical Theology and Christian Discipleship at Northwest Nazarene University. The original article in Chapter 4, entitled "Scripture As Formation: The Role of Scripture in Christian Formation," was authored by Richard P. Thompson and Mark A. Maddix. It appeared in the *Wesleyan Theological Journal*, vol. 46:1 (Spring 2011). Used by permission.

Philip R. Meadows, Ph.D. (University of Cambridge), is Lecturer in Missiology and Wesleyan Studies at Cliff College. He served as

President of the Wesleyan Theological Society. The article in Chapter 6 by Philip Meadows, titled "'Candidates for Heaven': Wesleyan Resources for a Theology of Religions," originally appeared in the *Wesleyan Theological Journal*, vol. 35:1 (Spring 2000). Used by permission.

Thomas E. Phillips, Ph.D. (Southern Methodist University), was Professor of New Testament and Early Christian Studies at Point Loma Nazarene University. He is web moderator of "Wesleyans in Theological Dialogue" (WTD). The original article in Chapter 14 by Thomas E. Phillips is titled "A Wesleyan Needle in a Cinematic Haystack: Seeking Sanctification in Contemporary Films." It appeared in the *Wesleyan Theological Journal*, vol. 41:2 (Fall 2006). Used by permission.

Cheryl J. Sanders, Th.D. (Harvard Divinity School), is Professor of Christian Ethics at Howard University School of Divinity and Senior Pastor of the Third Street Church of God in Washington, D.C. An exploration of this worship tradition in Chapter 16 originally appeared as the article by Cheryl J. Sanders titled "African-American Worship in the Pentecostal and Holiness Movements." It appeared in the *Wesleyan Theological Journal*, vol. 32:2 (Fall 1997). Used by permission.

John W. V. Smith, Ph.D. (University of Southern California), was historian of the Church of God (Anderson) and Professor of Church History and Associate Dean of Anderson University School of Theology. Chapter 18, "Holiness and Unity: Fulfilling the Prayers of Jesus," is a combination of John Smith's article, "Holiness and Unity," which appeared in the *Wesleyan Theological Journal*, vol. 10 (Spring 1975), and Gilbert Stafford's article, "Faith and Order: Holiness Church Participation," which appeared in vol. 32:1 (Spring 1997). The first section of this chapter is from Smith and the second from Stafford. Used by permission.

Timothy L. Smith, Ph.D. (Harvard University), was Professor of History, Director of the American Religious History doctoral program, and Chair of the Education Department at the Johns Hopkins University. The Smith/Wynkoop Book Award, given by the Wesleyan Theological Society, was named in part in his honor. The original article in Chapter 7 by Timothy L. Smith was entitled "John Wesley and the Second Blessing." It appeared in the *Wesleyan Theological Journal*, vol. 22:1-2 (1986). Used by permission.

Howard A. Snyder, Ph.D. (University of Notre Dame), was Professor of Wesley Studies at Tyndale Seminary and previously was Professor of the History and Theology of Mission in the E. Stanley Jones School of World Mission and Evangelism at Asbury Theological Seminary. Snyder served both as Secretary-Treasurer and President of the Wesleyan Theological Society, won the Smith/Wynkoop Book Award, and is a Lifetime Achievement Award winner. The original article in Chapter 2 by Howard A. Snyder was entitled "The Holy Reign of God." It appeared in the *Wesleyan Theological Journal*, vol. 24:1–2 (1989). Used by permission.

Gilbert W. Stafford, Th.D. (Boston University), was Professor of Systematic Theology, Associate Dean, and Dean of the Chapel of Anderson University School of Theology. Chapter 18, "Holiness and Unity: Fulfilling the Prayers of Jesus," is a combination of John Smith's article, "Holiness and Unity," which appeared in the *Wesleyan Theological Journal*, vol. 10 (Spring 1975), and Gilbert Stafford's article, "Faith and Order: Holiness Church Participation," which appeared in vol. 32:1 (Spring 1997). The first section of this chapter is from Smith and the second from Stafford. Used by permission.

Susie C. Stanley, Ph.D. (Iliff School of Theology/University of Denver), was Professor of Historical Theology in the Department of Biblical and Religious Studies at Messiah College. She served as

President of the Wesleyan Theological Society and is one of its Lifetime Achievement Award winners. Chapter 12 originally appeared in two articles by Susie Stanley. One is titled "Empowered Foremothers: Wesleyan/Holiness Women Speak to Today's Christian Feminists." It appeared in the *Wesleyan Theological Journal*, vol. 24:1–2 (1989). The other article is titled "'Tell Me The Old, Old Story': An Analysis of Autobiographies by Holiness Women." It appeared in the *Wesleyan Theological Journal*, 29:1–2 (Spring-Fall, 1994). Used by permission.

Merle D. Strege, Th.D. (Graduate Theological Union), is Historian of the Church of God (Anderson) and Professor of Historical Theology, having taught in the School of Theology and now in the Department of Religious Studies of Anderson University. The original article in Chapter 13 by Merle D. Strege was entitled "Holiness and Higher Education." It appeared in the *Wesleyan Theological Journal*, vol. 32.1 (Spring 1997). Used by permission.

Douglas M. Strong, Ph.D. (Princeton Theological Seminary), is Dean of the School of Theology and Professor of the History of Christianity at Seattle Pacific University. He served as President of the Wesleyan Theological Society and won the Smith/Wynkoop Book Award. The original article by Douglas Strong in Chapter 5 was titled "Sanctified Eccentricity: Continuing Relevance of the Nineteenth-Century Holiness Paradigm." It appeared in the *Wesleyan Theological Journal*, vol. 35:1 (Spring, 2000). Used by permission.

Richard P. Thompson, Ph.D. (Southern Methodist University), is Professor of New Testament, and has served as Chair of the Religion Department at Northwest Nazarene University. He is Book Editor and President-elect of the Wesleyan Theological Society. The original article in Chapter 4 was entitled "Scripture As Formation: The Role of Scripture in Christian Formation," and was authored by Richard P. Thompson and

Mark A. Maddix. It appeared in the *Wesleyan Theological Journal*, vol. 46:1 (Spring 2011). Used by permission.

Don Thorsen, Ph.D. (Drew University), is Professor of Theology and Chair of the Graduate Department of Religion and Ethics in the Azusa Pacific Graduate School of Theology at Azusa Pacific University. He served as President of the Wesleyan Theological Society.  The original article for Chapter 1 by Don Thorsen was entitled "Holiness Manifesto: An Ecumenical Document." It appeared in the *Wesleyan Theological Journal*, vol. 42:2 (2007). Used by permission. The original article for Chapter 9 by Don Thorsen was entitled "Ecumenism, Spirituality, and Holiness: Wesley and the Variety of Christian Spiritualities." It appeared in the *Wesleyan Theological Journal*, vol. 41:1 (2006). Used by permission. Dr. Thorsen is co-editor of this present volume.